VIBRANT
SELF-LEADERSHIP

Reinventing Ourselves to
Reinvent Our Organizations

NADIA JOYNSON

BALBOA.
PRESS

A DIVISION OF HAY HOUSE

Balboa Press books may be ordered through booksellers or by contacting:

Balboa Press
A Division of Hay House
1663 Liberty Drive
Bloomington, IN 47403
www.balboapress.com
1 (877) 407-4847

Print information available on the last page.

ISBN: 978-1-5043-7770-6 (sc)
ISBN: 978-1-5043-7771-3 (e)

Balboa Press rev. date: 04/07/2017

OUR GENERATION

To stand my ground, to be who I am
No more, no less, not a hologram

My light as a signal for all to behold
The power of my being, I let it unfold

As a token creation, to celebrate new
I am hope for what we choose to review

Dedicated to this generation of heart-centered leaders, this poem is you, may you have the courage to stand in your truth, to sow a new era on the foundations of respect of diversity, joy & connection.

Nadia Joynson, January 2017

CONTENTS

I'd like to thank...

With gratitude to all the wonderful people who have made my life such a colorful painting of diversity and richness through so many exchanges. If I have left you even the tiniest spark of love and possibility in return then I have already died a very happy lady. May the remainder simply *be* in joy together...

INTRODUCTION

When I was starting out in my research to support people to embody more collaborative behaviours, despite the fact that I have been an avid fan of holistic health and personal development since being a teenager, I never expected that it would turn into such a fascinating journey of discovery!

A few years ago, one impression that stayed with me strongly in reading *Reinventing Organizations* by Frederic Laloux was that there was a spiritual element to moving into a posture of transitioning to a new free enterprise, or 'Teal' organization as he defines it. *"Is that really necessarily so?"* I asked myself. Today I would reply to that with a resounding *"yes"*. In my search to define the behaviours required for self-leadership, I was shown many ways of being and realities. As I questioned and remained open to the learning that came my way, I started to see a vibrant picture of the way forward, combining both modern insights and approaches but also many linkages to past wisdom which is both simple and easily forgotten in our busy lives today. In turn I hope to share some of them with you through these pages, accompanied by both stories and practical examples. My intention is simply to share my learning and elements of the path that subsequently unfolded for me. In doing so, I share some of my own stories in the spirit of authenticity.

It was a deep frustration of mine as I left a role as Head of Learning for an international company that even in people-centred organizations, worries about leading people astray prevents many Human Resources teams from accompanying people in their search for wholeness. Despite my belief that we are already 'whole', part of this process involves recognizing our wounds and accepting all parts of ourselves, before we can move to self-realization. Inner work is seen as neither the responsibility nor allowed within most traditional corporate environments, none-the-less it is a necessary step on the path to self-leadership which essentially contains elements of connecting to one's true self. My belief is that any programme which doesn't encourage this connection to self will remain superficial and therefore ineffective. The paradox is that we want to empower people but we paternalistically say in this way that they are too influenceable and don't know what approaches might sit well with their own sense of self. Yet this is what self-leadership encourages of us, to know our truth. This book is thus intended to offer some possibilities as a bridge for those who wish to try new ways of being both individually and in togetherness on that journey to self-leadership. My belief is that until we reinvent ourselves through welcoming our wholeness, our organizations will not evolve. They will remain places where we do not feel we can fully be ourselves. We have a choice to take a deep look within to find our truths but then sharing them is fundamental. In doing so we can live by them in authenticity and also build trustful relationships as an enabler to reinventing those organisations bottom-up in ways that allow each individual to share their full potential and true vibrant natures. No masks, no fear.

I also believe that every person is a leader and that we need less hierarchical and separating definitions of the term to become widespread. I spent a lot of time trying to find programmes which would support the development of leadership capabilities but could never really find much that wasn't elitist and/or only results focused, targeting a chosen few. Personally, it was never ok for me to segregate an organization in this way.

I wanted to focus on the experiential aspects, the stories that we all pull through in life to realize and develop our strengths, and the gifts we find in ourselves that make us the wonderful, heart-centred leaders that we are all capable of being. This might also explain my interest in the notion of self-leadership, which starts with each individual. Fortunately things are evolving, and there are now some great organizations and methods of peer-to-peer learning appearing to support self-realisation at all levels.

Each person has leadership qualities to bring to a team, family or organization. Any group needs to demonstrate different behaviours depending on their current context. Sometimes it's about providing direction but a lot of the time other less talked about behaviours such as supportiveness, a sense of humour, clarity, or organizational skills will prime. No one person has all of these at one time and neither are we islands which is why we need others. Diverse teams bring better results for this reason. We need to recognize and make use of everyone's gifts.

Discovering our true gifts, however, requires self-knowledge. When we get beyond the personality tests and basic personal development trainings, this depth of simply knowing helps us manoeuvre difficulties in a way these tools cannot. Our spirit provides our compass so that we may lead ourselves with integrity and authenticity.

Like a lot of people now in the area of free enterprise, I don't believe in associating people with titles or certificates. During my journey I have met a lot of amazing self-taught people who are doing equally amazing work. For me, within the question of assigning roles and respect for diversity, it's just as important to recognize the full breadth of what people can bring to the group, particularly from experience. Knowing something theoretically versus having inside understanding and compassion for a subject are totally different things. We hide behind the former too often to feel credible and neglect the latter to our detriment.

So to many, the idea of emerging, flatter forms of organization providing clarity and individual freedom to act is enticing. It looks great on paper. The thought that this could come without any consideration or support for how we might interact or actually connect together on a deeper personal level was a real question for me. The key to project success has always been the people involved. I've also long been fascinated by the balance between personal freedom and our interdependence. Whilst these modes of organization are unleashing our potential through empowering roles, what is still not sufficiently prevalent is talk of how to develop the behaviours of fully taking the responsibility for our empowerment and also this interdependency. This is harder than just delegating, it's about choosing sovereignty. Setting out, it was even unclear as to what these behaviours should be and who should define them in this new context. Values are demonstrated bottom up, whatever the corporate brochure says. What is clear to me is that a leader who is conscious cannot ignore the impact that his or her actions have on another person, whether inside or outside an organization. With that clarity comes choice.

And what of moving away from so much attention on results? What does this shift suggest about how we operate together? In this period of history where we are all learning to live with uncertainty, feeling our way forward is key. Logic has its place but it is also vital now to develop our intuition and our ability to listen and see our realities deeply. Over and above this, a true sense of the concepts of working with trust, unity and shared intention indeed requires a deeper sense of knowing, both of ourselves and where the collective might wish to go. A process of surrendering to, but also being conscious of what is emerging. This is not passive. To the contrary, we can only do this when we are wholly present to, and look fearlessly at the present. In doing so, and embracing the opportunities that self-leadership bring, what a beautiful collective unfolding awaits us.

MOUNT ETNA:
LISTENING DEEPLY TO LIFE

That morning we were up at dawn, excited about perhaps seeing an amazing sunrise. I'd spontaneously agreed to join a small group who would be walking up Mount Etna. *"Ok why not"* I thought. The weather wasn't great but I wasn't in Catania for long and it would be a shame to miss the opportunity. That morning I sensed life was conspiring to allow me to experience my strength.

The small group ended up being just three people after one person dropped out because of the weather. As we arrived at the foot of Etna, I saw the approaching challenge. Or rather I didn't as the beautiful countryside was wrapped in a blanket of mist from what was probably a few hundred metres in altitude upwards. *"How long to the top?"* I asked. *"Probably like 5 hours"* was the reply. *"5 hours?! Seriously?"* I sighed. What was initially an idea of a short morning uphill stroll was turning into a rather more imposing possibility. *"Well ok, here we go"* I thought, *"nothing else planned today!"*.

As we were preparing to leave the car I took everything I didn't need out of my bag. Better to travel light! As time has gone by and I've developed a stronger inner world I find that I don't need to take so much with me when I travel. Sure I like my comforts but the more you know yourself the more you know exactly what to take and what you can find in the environment around you, the fears of lack disperse. Lighten the load I thought, we already carry enough heaviness with us. Take the minimum but take your sense of humour.

So off we went. As we approached the start of the trail, the thought of taking the cable car really was tempting I have to admit. But then i'd agreed to walk with the group. As we set out, it quickly became evident that we all had the same intention but we didn't quite see the *"how"* of the climb in the same way. The young guy we were with zoomed off, first a few metres ahead and then sure enough within half an hour he was out of view.

"Interesting how predictable that was" I thought. What is it about being young that you can just tell they either have something to prove or they're just impatient. What do you do with a group when one of them just has no wish to walk with the rest? Give them a responsibility to check the way ahead then come and report to the others? Open the way, check the direction? It certainly has it's benefits that someone strives, takes initiatives and has autonomy. What is it about youth that makes them believe that they're invincible, that's useful to those who've slowed with age. He had no thought at all that he wouldn't be capable. We'll see in a while, I decided quite simply to pace myself. It was a strange feeling being the slowest of the group for once as it's not my nature. Humbling and at the same time a reminder to take in what I was seeing on the way up. The important thing was to pace myself, to go at what I knew to be my own speed. I would have the experience that I needed and see some of the environment around me that perhaps I might not otherwise notice.

As we winded up the rocky track, I fairly quickly realized that by walking in the footprints that others had made before me my ascension was much easier. It reminded me of learning from the experience of those who have walked a path before you. Of course our experience is unique but we can learn a lot and thus find a firmer foothold if we listen well. The same goes of remaining aware. At one point I was tired and it just so happened that I hit on a rough spot. Quite rocky but the loose kind that takes that bit more effort to manoeuvre and balance at the same time. I was psyching myself to persevere and find a second wind when my inner voice said " look to the side". As I did so I saw that the path was more even so I gratefully switched. This happened again perhaps a few hundred metres further up. Again I was looking at the path in front of me which seemed the most direct. The guide I was with could see I was tiring again and said to me kindly "hey, if you move to the left it looks like it might be a little easier". He was right. Gratefully I moved. On the third occasion my perception was much wider and I saw the option myself. Sometimes we need prompts from outside. Small nudges that remind us humbly that we don't have all of the answers to see everything ourselves all of the time. We all have different perspectives of any given situation and our experience. If we insist on our track or go it alone, it's highly likely to be a tougher journey.

In the same grain, this kind guide of mine actually offered to carry my bag for me. It wasn't too heavy but I reminded myself that indeed he was clearly stronger than me and that if he was offering why would I not accept? Being weaker is a position that we can learn from. What about those team or family members who are learning or want to progress, how do we help them? He wasn't breaking my self-respect or my autonomy. The only thing that could make me refuse in this circumstance was pride. So I thankfully accepted, reminding myself that he was probably happy to help me out too. We are all different, so we're strong in some circumstances and weaker in others and it is important to have the humility to recognize this fact in order to both appreciate other's gifts and let them into our world which requires vulnerability. A deep act of humanity which we can only attain by overcoming our fears of rejection and incompleteness.

At what must have been about 2000 feet we sat down again to rest. Since there was heavy mist around us I didn't even realize it was raining! I reached into my pocket, put on a hat and felt much cosier. Simplicity to identify a need, satisfy it and be back to that space of calm again. I looked around and saw, not so far into the distance, but the immediate nature around me. Then a reminder to listen into the stillness. I had been so busy walking that I had not experienced the vastness of the outside stillness. The environment felt like a deep balance between the masculine and the feminine. The rock, the strength, stamina, the timeless presence of the mountain, versus the gentleness, the mystical and transitory nature of the mist just caressing the hillside. Like a blanket, nurturing, enveloping. The contrast reigned in the silence and I felt a renewal of energy to go on. How often we forget about nature's ability to uplift and resource when we are advancing so courageously on our paths. Quality time and connection, not necessarily quantity.

Around the time we set off again, I was also reminded of the fact that we are much stronger than we think. Human resilience has been proven so many times. My soul didn't engineer for me to be here by accident. If it thought I could handle this feat then I certainly could. Life never puts things in our path that we can't handle if we stay connected to our beliefs in ourselves and indeed in that higher good. Who am I to contradict? I'm on this path for a reason. Let's do it. Let's keep engaging with it.

At probably around 2900 feet we arrived at a platform where there was a restaurant, and of course the arrival of the cable car. I felt quite proud of myself for having taken the harder option this time and the snack felt so much better than I imagine it would have done had I taken the easy route!

We had a choice at this stage to keep going to the top or to call it a day. We estimated that it would take around one and a half hours more to the top but that just as we arrived there and subsequently started our descent it was likely to be getting dark. Part of me wanted to go on, to prove that I could do it, to keep building on the positive frame of reference, my new-found experience of strength, that I'd constructed during the day. But my intuition told me that the best would be to start our descent. Surely I could learn more but I had achieved what I had set out to do for the day in experiencing my strength. I certainly would not enjoy walking down at night and indeed it may even be risky since we had no torches. Again I was reminded of the principle of "*just good enough*". We were there.

On the way back down, unsurprisingly I underestimated the track. Of course walking down was easier so we could go more quickly! Still take it slowly and watch where you place your feet. "*Stay vigilant because it's easy to make mistakes when we're being nonchalant*" said my inner voice. It also reminded me of when we dig down into our shadow aspects, to do so kindly and with care. To stay objective, not get caught up in the stories we tell ourselves. These explorations are easier when we know the route and we can recognize when we're stumbling and have the humility to know that it's ok to slip. It is also important to keep in mind the ascent we made. There is no duality, just a scale of what we can discover about ourselves.

Even if I was paying attention I slipped on several occasions on the way down as the paths were covered with small rocks and it was fairly steep. On the first occasion, I found my balance again and I thought of times I had supported other people and I thought "*yes, perhaps someone else will be there to catch me*". As I did so I slipped again and it really felt like a message to say, "no, you gave that willingly, there is no obligation to replicate. There can be no expectations or animosity when we're in that space. Just do what you feel is right". You are responsible for what you choose to give and receive in any moment. No obligations to replicate in the space of self-leadership and indeed of love itself. Being neutral in this way also avoids us getting caught up so often in other's projections of needs and desires.

Halfway down as I saw the cable cars sailing by, I asked myself why people were even going up there today by cable car? What did they see? It wasn't possible to see far at all because of the heavy mist. It occurred to me in that moment that they had perhaps been on a similar journey but seen nothing, although obviously I don't know what their actual experiences were. The contrast was just there to make me feel grateful to have taken a path where I had seen myself, even if it wasn't possible to experience the whole view around me in this instant. As we neared the foot of Etna, I thanked God for the experience and the smallest, white feather floated in front of me. This has always been a sign of encouragement for me of progressing on my path, that I am supported by a force bigger than me.

As we got into the car, it started to rain heavily so I was particularly grateful for avoiding that. But where was the young guy? We'd tried to call and text. No answer. We waited for two hours patiently assuming that he had walked to the summit then slowly began to wonder if he had even decided to head back into Catania. As the sun began to set, we started to ask questions to the personnel about security and tracking possibilities. It was at that moment that the guide saw him wandering, tired and a little disorientated, back into the car park from another path. He had indeed managed to walk over the top and then lost his bearings on the way back down. No harm done but just good enough to make me thankful to have avoided such a detour, having listened to my intuition. This is no judgement of his journey, it was simply a different one that day. He was being the pioneer and whatever his experience, one universal truth is that through stepping out of our comfort zones and through mistakes we learn. Perhaps I could have learnt more, who knows, it's all about choice.

That day I listened carefully to that calm inner voice and in doing so rediscovered my strength. We need to make time to find stillness in order to connect to all the wisdom that is around us. Whatever our context may be, life is always trying to share something positive with us.

THE FOUR PILLARS OF
SELF-LEADERSHIP

When I'm asked about my programmes, I find myself invariably describing them through the four pillars : Calm, Connect, Collaborate, Create.

Self-Leadership is about fundamentally owning one's reality, along with the related responsibility to oneself and others. This means recognising and acting on the corresponding choices we have at any moment in order to empower ourselves. Making responsible, loving choices from the point of view of oneself and the collective is an adult thing to do. On this basis, we fundamentally need to learn to "parent" ourselves so that the choices we are making are not driven by reactions, the projections that we place on others, or dictated by the world around us. This is why it's about *being* before *doing*. Our foundations of self-mastery provide a solid basis on which we can build many wonderful creations together. Investing in ourselves, like everything else is a choice. If you're ready to make that choice then this book is for you.

People who are self-leading are :

- Conscious and mindful
- Intentional and authentic
- Looking for simplicity

- Emotionally balanced (objective in their chosen courses of action and in doing so compassionate with themselves and others)
- Aware of their responsibilities to themselves and their impact on others

Their choices are made from a place of centredness, linking heart and head.

Here we talk about how to do that by developing ourselves through the four key domains of : *Calm, Connect, Collaborate,* and *Create.* Each builds on another so that when we find a state of inner calm and truly connect to know ourselves, we can then meet others in a more authentic way. Even with the best of intentions, however, it can be useful to look to how we are interacting with others to collaborate and create together in order that we can do so more fluidly and for the benefit of all.

The schema below shows how these domains are interdependent and the potential outcomes of integrating these practices in our lives :

POTENTIAL OUTCOMES

CALM

Awareness, presence,
clarity, consciousness
Well-being

CONNECT

Self-knowledge &
satisfying own needs
Emotional balance
Realizing our uniqueness
& sovereignty

COLLABORATE

Positive
interdependency
Respect for diversity
Community spirit

CREATE

Enhancing flow states
Managing uncertainty
Working in partnership
to emerge the new

In support of these four areas, here is a summary of some of the approaches we will be looking at together.

Calm : I make space for myself

Tools :

- *Mindfulness (inner world work)*
- *Beginner's mind*
- *Developing Intuition*

Connect : I switch myself on!

Tools :

- *Knowing one's values & strengths*
- *Beliefs, feelings & contrast work*
- *Dharma: Walking the talk with discipline*

Collaborate : I connect deeply with others

Tools :

- *Dialogue & storytelling*
- *Trust building exercises*
- *Non-violent communication*

Create : We co-create our future

Tools :

- *SCAMPER & journaling*
- *Developing intuition & surrender*
- *Co-creation frameworks that are minimal, supportive and engage all parties*

These are just some of the tools that could support these areas. The lists are not exhaustive, but I happen to like self-help techniques, especially given that we're talking about personal empowerment through self-leadership. I share them here as a starting point because I found some of these approaches were not discussed openly or placed in the context of how they could be useful supports in moments of deep transition. They are suggestions to move us into the realm of other possibilities. In your discovery process you may find that something else works better for you and that's perfect. Indeed, since we are all unique and have our individual journeys, this is a key question to ask ourselves at each stage : What do I want to develop and why? How does that feel for me? Does it work for me? We can't listen to ourselves enough. We need to question in order to find our unique response and in doing so assert our sovereignty.

During my interactions with many trainers and therapists we have often talked of the importance of seeing every journey as unique and continuous. It is never about just the impact that one person makes, but how we all support each other to discover ourselves along our unfolding lives.

My intention in sharing these stories is that they may be of service in providing one or two steps along someone's path. I spent a while collecting other people's beautiful stories, until a close friend suggested that since I was writing about authenticity and wholeness, perhaps I should share some of mine. This is therefore an open sharing of my experience in the true spirit of authenticity. I therefore have no aim to convince, to be right or wrong, only to share what I have learnt. I do so with love and that you may receive whatever works for you.

CALM

Many great spiritual writers and teachers over time have talked about the importance of finding our inner calm. Our soul is quiet. It does not need to shout to be of importance, its victories do not come from domination, arrogance or any other fear-based responses. It requires us to pause to look inside instead of concentrating on external influences and events. To be a good captain of our ship, we need to be able to navigate through both calm and turbulent times, this is where our inner compass is key.

Even in a more practical way, a flight attendant will talk about putting on your own oxygen mask first before attending to others. This can seem counter-intuitive to many, especially parents and those in caring professions, until we become so exhausted through continually giving without concern for ourselves, that we find that we don't recognize ourselves anymore. Everyone has an energetic space and a physical body that needs to regenerate. More importantly we cannot evolve spiritually if we are in a state of fight or flight. We need time to just be, to feel and to reflect. According ourselves these moments on a regular basis will not only increase well-being but also open us up to a world of discovery. This stillness is an indispensable starting point in the journey of seeing who we are and what we wish to truly share.

Breathing through fear

In the Native American tradition, a sweat lodge is a communal practice which provides a means of purification, both physical and spiritual. It's like an intensive sauna created by bringing red hot stones into an enclosed space and pouring water on them which is said to purify and heal. Those who are versed in the deep spirituality of this practice I hope will forgive my simplification for the purposes of illustration here. I was invited by a friend to attend one for the weekend. It is not something that I had ever considered doing but being openminded, as usual, events conspired to ensure I was free to participate and I accepted life's offering.

As we arrived on the grounds, I could straight away feel the stillness and peace of the surroundings. It was quite a vast domain that is regularly used for such practices. We sat down to eat a vegetarian meal in a very simple restaurant, and as it was late we were the only ones there. We chatted happily and subsequently headed back to our respective dormitories to rest for the night. As I looked around my sparse and frankly quite cold room I began to wonder what I was doing there rather than enjoying the warmth and comfort of my own home. The steel bunkbeds were no match, and especially not when only 30 minutes later, I started to feel very queasy. I ended up awake almost the whole night very ill. By morning I was drained, not in a great mood and wondering if I should take the next train home. As it happened we were very far from any station so I finally resigned myself, a little begrudgingly, to stay and see how things progressed. I tried as much as possible to listen to the talks about Native American ways of life, the respect they have not just for nature but for Wakane itself, this force of unity, the infinite around us that they see as indescribable.

As the sweat lodge ceremony was coming to an opening, I thought, *"well I haven't come all this way to not participate"*. I decided to enter, do my best and not judge, just let the experience be what it needed to be.

The hut is typically positioned with the entrance to the east. Inside, each of the four rounds of purification are represented by a direction. Firstly the black West to which we ask for support from our guides. Then to the white North where the characteristics of courage, honesty, strength, cleanliness and endurance are recognized. On to the red East in which we recognize the knowledge and individual prayer which we ask will lead us to wisdom. The finally, the direction of the yellow South which symbolizes growth and healing. A culmination of all of the journey through the other directions. What is beautiful is that all notions of race, color and religion are set aside as we enter this place of spiritual and physical purification and growth. An interesting aspect, however, is that my journey had clearly started as soon as I set foot in the grounds, hence my illness.

As the ceremony started, we entered the lodge one by one each saying Ahu or Ahé depending on our sex as in accordance with tradition. Everyone sits in a circle around the heated stones in the centre which are said to represent the spirits of the grandparents of those present (the Tunkashilas). As the temperature cools down, more stones are brought in little by little accompanied by a respectful display of welcome.

As the entrance was closed for the first time I felt my stomach turn slightly. Let's see I thought. It was feeling almost cosy and very communal until the group started to play several drums simultaneously. It is quite a strange feeling already, sitting in the pitch black, only feeling the ground below you. A bit like like being in a void. You're held by nothing, so you might be able to imagine how people's inner child gets triggered. The drums were so loud and combined with everyone singing, the vibration went through me in such a deep way that I felt extremely dizzy, especially with the intense heat. So much so that I viscerally knew in an instant that I was going to pass out. I tried to reach out for support from the lady beside me who brushed off my touch in almost a brusque reaction (it appears she was having difficulty too). In that instant I was alone, face to face with my fear. If I passed out no-one would even know and I felt decidedly panicked given the fact that I was ill. I had two choices, try to scramble for the door or stay with it to see what happened. And at that moment my inner voice whispered to me to *"lie down and sing"*. As I lay down I felt some relief both from the coldness and reassurance of the earth, but my mental patterns stepped in. *"I don't know the words"* I pleaded. *"Just sing, it doesn't matter"* was the reply *"don't forget that we are with you, you are well surrounded"*. Sure enough as I let myself flow the words came to me. They may not have been exact, I have no recollection but I suddenly didn't feel out of place. I was being gently rocked in their heady melody, connected to a vital force stronger than me and I was being helped by the feeling of community. *"You always have your place at any moment"* I heard. *"Let go and you will see how you can be enchanted"*.

"Have patience. Things come in gentleness and at the right time" my inner voice told me. Indeed, as the different doors progressed, people shared in beautiful, authentic dialogue whatever pains, requests or gratitude needed to surface. It became a beautiful moment of authentic sharing.

This was quite an unexpected but very moving experience for me to learn in particular how we can surpass the fear that our mind plays out. Breathing deeply, being wholly in the moment, surrendering to feeling the experience, and connecting with others are absolutely key to facing many of our fears and in so doing letting life in. We can look past the fear to the love that is always behind it, helping us to grow.

For a moment I felt just a glimpse of what it must have felt like to be a proud, courageous squaw with her presence and connection to Mother Earth. A wonderful lesson and I am grateful to life for having allowed me, yet again, to experience the profound wisdom of another harmony-focused culture.

As life does, the integration of my lesson was tested on a flight not long afterwards when I suddenly felt nauseous. Since this is not a common occurrence for me, I immediately thought of the lodge and told myself, *"It's mind over matter, stay in the present and breathe"*. In no time at all it had passed and I was feeling proud of having grown and applied my new techniques.

Building Presence

Are you aware of what you are you consciously choosing in any moment and why? Do you notice the details of your surroundings and the people who are with you? Being present in the moment takes regular practice. Outside of any religion or culture, it is cultivating our awareness to avoid our minds acting like untrained puppies in order that we can connect to our inner stillness.

There is a big movement to encourage us to slow our lives down and for good reason. Connectivity can be a very positive thing but as a support in order to make our lives easier. If it starts to become excessive then we could be losing out on many activities that will help us to feel better and more connected to who we are on the inside. It is most definitely possible to tame the social media monster so that it doesn't take over our lives! These sections will talk therefore, not about squeezing more activities into our lives but streamlining them in order that we make time for those that are beneficial to our well-being.

Some simple suggestions you can try out in order to start slowing down:

Breathe : Do you notice yourself rushing from one activity to another, or notice feelings of anxiety or overwhelm arise from the amount of things you feel you need to complete or achieve? Then before launching into the next item, stop and take a deep breath. Seeing your stomach go in and out as you breathe is a great sign that you are breathing deeply. When we are stressed we breathe more shallowly and from the chest. Take another couple of breaths while you just stand or sit in stillness.

Do one thing at a time : We might be capable of doing a number of things in parallel over a short space of time but that doesn't make it good for us, nor ensure we do them well. Try focusing on one of the items which will bring the most impact to your life or is urgent, rather than simply the last issue or request that came up. Make time for the things that are important to you and be focused as you do them. The rest can wait!

Slow down intentionally : When you notice yourself rushing through an activity, simply stop purposefully and then take it up again in a less rushed and more deliberate way. Sometimes we don't realize how quickly we're working or speeding up to get things done. In slowing an activity down, you may do slightly less but the chances are that you will do it better and your body and mind will also thank you for it!

Several years ago I was rushing to work one morning as usual, thinking about my huge 'to-do' list. As I arrived, a colleague (who had noticed me as he had driven past) kindly striking up some light conversation with me, asked if I had seen the little boy and the dog playing together outside the front of the office? "*Wasn't it sweet?*" he enquired. I was at the same time both embarrassed and filled with surprise as I realized that I must have walked straight past them without even seeing them, let alone appreciating the fun moment that they must have been enjoying together. *"Wow, was I so lost in my thoughts?"* Well, yes. That was a powerful lesson to me to make a conscious effort to be present to the moment I'm faced with, giving my full attention to whatever I happen to be doing, the person I am with and/or to my experience of life. This takes practice as our minds wander very easily. We may dwell on thoughts or worries rather than addressing them only at the time that we can actually do something about them.

Try alternating these small exercises to continue building awareness of your inner and outer worlds :

Mindful of the outside : As you wake up, just lie in bed for another two minutes listening to the noises around you. What do you notice?

Mindful of the inside : As you wake up, for two minutes, notice how you feel and if there are any places in your body where you notice a particular sensation, stiffness, or perhaps even discomfort? Place your attention on that area or that feeling. What do you notice?

How Can Mindfulness Help Me?

When we are conscious about what we are thinking or the way we are behaving, we give ourselves the power to change anything that doesn't suit us. And I mean pretty much anything. But sometimes it's hard to know where to start because we don't talk openly about a lot of really effective approaches, many of which are also freely available to us. They are intended to help us bridge the gap between our inside and outside so our actions and statements out in the world aren't superficial, but represent a real means of developing personal power and transformation through conscious choice.

The practice of Mindfulness helps take us back to first principles to see where we are placing our attention (and therefore using our energy) at any moment in time.

Jon Kabat-Zinn, the founder of the world famous Mindfulness Based Stress Reduction (MBSR) programme defines mindfulness as *"paying attention in a particular way, on purpose, in the present moment, and non-judgementally"*. Why would I want to do that? Well, essentially because developing a sense of inner calm also brings clarity. If my mind is on auto-pilot then I'm reacting to events, rather than consciously choosing my response. With choice comes personal leadership.

Starting with tools such as Mindfulness is like cleaning up and maintaining a dam upstream rather than patching up the problems of flooding and deluge downstream. When we leave our minds open to harmful thoughts they can cause us to play out repetitive and un-helpful patterns. One such pattern could be impulsive behaviours such as eating when we feel down and then realising we don't really feel better at all. Like a torch, mindfulness helps us to pay attention and in doing so shines a light on these thoughts and choices. Thoughts are like bait. If we focus too much attention on them then they hook us in and we ruminate them. Most are superfluous. This is why it can be a very good idea not to follow the news too closely. It has the same effect of continuously reinforcing our thoughts with fear and negativity. The search for inner peace causes many to distance themselves from this need to be constantly connected, to abstract from the drama. We don't need it. Not only does it maintain our physiology in a state of stress but it also keeps us locked into the fear-based mentality of right/wrong, good/bad, us/them separation. Instead we are looking for the silent awareness between these thoughts. The sense of knowing and connection that is the true self.

So the mindset change which sets off a positive chain reaction is to believe that you can choose and have the will to put in place some very first small changes in your life to incorporate these moments of calm which will little by little have a very positive impact. Time and again we might say to ourselves *"that's just the way I am"* or *"if only"*. Mindfulness is an invitation to explore other possibilities. That there is perhaps another way to see the world which brings both strength in choice and peace of mind. Strive for your own inner peace as being more important than anything else. The first step is to accept that all the change that you want to see comes from you. Instead of wanting to change others or the world around us we start by simply being with what is, welcoming our reality as it is. You are the key, and the prize is freeing your mind and your beautiful potential. It's there for the taking, no one is preventing you but yourself.

There are many ways to be mindful in our day-to-day. The important thing is to exercise the practice of placing our attention on whatever we are doing in an intentional way. It means that we are in the moment wholly and not thinking about the past, the next event coming up or our to-do list. We can be more in a state of feeling than thinking. A state of presence and flow can be achieved with certain activities in the same way. Gardening, praying, listening to music, walking are just a few.

If you'd like to be accompanied to learn Mindfulness then there are lots of great MBSR teachers around now and the 8-week programme has been the subject of many evaluations. There are also some good applications to start to learn to be Mindful, including at the time of press Headspace, Zazen, Mindfulness For Beginners (Jon Kabat-Zinn), Mind, and Petit Bambou. They'll help you build up your practice each day, little by little.

Even starting with just a few minutes each day is great. In order to feel the benefits, however, you do need to make your practice a regular occurrence, but it's worth persisting. So try investing five minutes of the time that you'd normally spend perhaps on surfing online with five minutes of Mindfulness each day. With some patience you can perhaps increase your practice to twenty minutes per day and in time, you may feel that you don't know how you managed without this precious *"me-time"*! The key thing to remember is not to try to set results or expectations for yourself, simply use the time to just *be*.

The Importance of A 'Beginner's Mind'

Taking time out to integrate calming and/or mindful practices into our lives enhance our well-being and build awareness. We become more aware of our thoughts and behaviours over time. That they are not *us* but rather just passing through us, a little like watching traffic on a road in front of us. We can therefore choose to keep them or change them with a little intention once we cultivate our awareness.

As these practices bring clarity, we can also start to identify some of our patterns, perhaps the a priori that I hold when I'm coming at an issue or an encounter with anyone. I'm not in a space of real clarity and open to receiving new information when I am driven by these influences. These patterns or *a priori* represent our mental maps of the world and they impose some judgement on the situation we face. We could perhaps instead just let the moment unfold, trying to look at it with fresh eyes every time, especially if I already know the person. It is vital to leave a space for the dialogue or an event to evolve, to learn something new, to grow, instead of presuming that we see the same situation and perhaps outcome over again.

Here are two exercises that you can try in order to help with suspending judgement and interpretation and also to avoid interrupting when someone else speaks :

- Count to 8 slowly in your mind as someone is speaking to you (this helps to calm the wish to jump in and make remarks or preempt what they say)
- Spend a few minutes consciously breathing before an event before a conversation. Place your attention on your heart-space and breathe in for the count of five and out for the count of five. When we do this for a few minutes we move into a state of *coherence* which helps us to calm and encourages the body to move into a parasympathetic state of recovery instead of operating in fight or flight mode. We can be more in a state of presence to the moment when calm, allowing us to focus on listening and feeling.

It takes humility to suspend our opinions and not impose what we think we know. Often we rush in and forget how much we can gain from maintaining a perspective of innocence. Rather, we can worry about feelings of vulnerability that it may bring, of perhaps looking naive or exposing oneself to another's position of superiority should they think know something better than we do. These are just judgements that we place on ourselves. Apart from learning more by being more receptive, we are also developing the capacity to see the beauty and cultivate acceptance of what is actually in front of us in every moment.

To conclude, when we are practicing awareness and operating in our own stories (and not other people's), we act with clarity and integrity. In this way our energy is not dispersed and our actions become impactful. As calm settles in our hearts and minds, we greet that stillness more willingly to start listening to our bodies and our precious inner voices. This allows them to guide our lives with more grace.

Compassion & Gratitude

It would not be complete to discuss Mindfulness practices and not talk about compassion. Connecting to our inner worlds move us from our heads to our hearts. We become less concerned with the drama of the outside when we know of the stillness to be found in any moment. In that stillness our hearts remind us of the true nature and depth of our being. To find this, we are asked to give up what we think we know.

It is between the breaths that we discover the true self. This is the essence that we are here to share, not the busy, stressed and anxious roles that we have created. This provides us with sovereignty and the possibility to honor the fullness of our being which comes through the magnificence of the heart, not the projections of the head. It is the strength of the heart field that connects us together to all things and therefore helps us to both find our sense of belonging and our compassion in seeing our inherent similarities with others. Without connecting to our humanity in this way, Mindfulness practices are simply ways of training our attention, our focus. As we welcome our own humanity, we become open to welcoming that of those around us.

Gratitude practice is also an excellent way to open our hearts. Reminding ourselves of what is good about our lives enables us to see the positive in the present. It limits our need to live in wishful thinking for the future, or the nostalgia of the past.

For the next 21 days, create a list adding one of the following elements to it (aim to recall that special person or moment as you write it down: *Where were you? How did you feel?*) :

- A message or post I received that made me smile or laugh
- A Person who helped me or I appreciate

- Something I learnt this week
- A nice thing that happened to me or just fell into place
- A moment I enjoyed or that inspired me
- Some good news or a positive surprise I received
- Something I achieved or an opportunity that came my way

When we notice things to be grateful for and we re-live positive experiences it's nourishing to our hearts. Neuroscience tells us that the brain has more difficulty memorising successes than it does the events that we consider failures. This is why positive psychology encourages us to remind ourselves regularly of these lighter and brighter moments. When we are conscious of them we can also invite life to send even more of the things that delight us by saying thank you.

Before starting the journey of connecting more deeply to our essence and gaining perspective on our intentions, let's take a pause to look at the practice of journaling.

Why is journaling useful?

Writing down our thoughts and describing our feelings can be a very powerful tool.

Noting whatever comes to our minds can help us to be conscious of what we are ruminating and the associated emotions that we may be suppressing. When we are conscious of a negative thought pattern and perhaps also the corresponding behaviour, we have the power to change it. To make a different choice. When journaling regularly, even just a few lines, we can look back and see the progress we've made which can be both motivating and fulfilling. Sometimes we forget to congratulate ourselves for the progress we make.

Journaling our feelings represents another dimension in this exploration. Whether written or through art, it brings form to sensations that we may otherwise have difficulty identifying or we may even try to ignore as we are going about our busy days. Describing them in this way (which can be, for example, through associating colors, or objects, or actions to them) externalizes the emotion, helping it to release and reminding us that we are not controlled by our emotions. They are reactions that are just passing through the body but which serve a useful purpose. By recognising them for their real purpose we can firstly, listen to what they are communicating to us without being submerged e.g. by anger or sadness and secondly, not be bound to them so strongly that we believe ourselves to be them, for example "I'm just an angry person, I can't help it". Our internal self talk loves to label ourselves in this way and in our journals we can see that we are a whole range of thoughts and feelings. That's just perfect because that is what it means to be a human being!

Finally, journaling is a great exercise to encourage us to love ourselves more. When we allow ourselves to write whatever comes without judging it, we learn to treat ourselves the same way, more freely. This is not always an easy exercise but well worth persevering!

So now that we've looked at why we might journal, lets take a first look at how we can get started together.

Journaling steps to get started:

- Find a space where I can write calmly
- Listen for my feelings
- What can I compare my feelings to?
- Select colors and words to represent my feelings
- What patterns do I see?

Explanation of each step in more detail:

1   Try to ensure that you have at least 10-20 minutes available in a place where you are least likely to be interrupted. Open your journal on a new page (this will ensure you are not influenced by your last entry!)

2   Before starting to write, take a moment of calm (perhaps using one of the exercises of Mindfulness or breathing) to let yourself notice any feelings.

3   Let yourself start to think about how you might describe those feelings, perhaps with an image, or a word, or perhaps an object like a cloud. This is telling you how the feeling may wish to be expressed. Is it dark and heavy? Perhaps pink and light? Blue and fluid? Try not to judge what comes to mind, you are just giving form to the emotion.

4   What colored pen would best represent the feeling? Now you can start to put this down on the page, perhaps by doodling the image or object, or by writing. You may want to write about the event that generated the feeling or just describe the feeling itself. Let yourself continue to write or draw whatever comes to you without trying to understand why. It can be a great to switch colors in the middle of your drawing or writing if another feeling comes up.

5   It is not necessary to arrive at any particular objective when journaling, but if you notice any observations about how your feelings changed or not, or perhaps conclusions or ideas for action around the subject of your journaling entry then note them down at the end. For example, *"I was really mad at Julia for the whole afternoon. Perhaps if I had asked her straight away why she didn't call me then I would have known earlier that she had a problem. I would not have assumed that she didn't want to speak to me. Next time I'll just ask"*

What else?

If one day you are not sure what to write then take a big marker pen and write in big letters "I don't know what to write today and it doesn't matter!!!". Let yourself feel that it's ok to not know sometimes. You can keep writing whatever comes to mind after this, or keep drawing squares or circles or stars or triangles...

It is not always easy to start journaling because we can wonder what to write. What could be interesting? How much to write? Finding the time in busy schedules is also tough. These are all judgements which we tell ourselves (sort of as if someone might be reading our journal). It is just for us, there is no right or wrong. Let yourself talk about anything and everything! Three pages a day is absolutely great but again just write freely until you feel like stopping, it's the regularity which helps us get into a state of flow. Once again, a lot of people who journal regularly attest to these moments being very mindful, almost meditative. Journaling your thoughts and feelings on the exercises throughout this book will support more you in developing more clarity around the patterns you are experiencing. Regularity brings progress.

The ability to develop our space of inner calm paves the way for more discovery of our true selves, away from the influence of the external world. Not only is it good for our well-being through reducing anxiety, depression and many other ailments, but it also reminds us of our real sovereignty as human beings. Our inner freedom. I am a huge believer in free will and the fact that through Mindful practices we can see more clearly the breadth of our possibilities in any moment, which is ultimately extremely empowering.

CONNECT

In finding ourselves, we are often hoping to do two things: know our truth and find our purpose. Building awareness supports us to connect into our inner world and to learn to listen. All of our truths are inside us. Being in a place of self-leadership means fundamentally standing in one's truth i.e. knowing and feeling deeply what our truth is and sharing it with the world.

Are you being your own guru? As with any walks of life, there is no dogma that's right and we can learn from many different teachers (we are all teachers by the way). So create your own philosophy out of the knowledge and experience you have gathered but most importantly according to what *feels* right to you. We're looking to be bold, whilst at the same time being conscious and coherent in the statements you make about yourself to the world. And above all else enjoy the journey of connecting to your essence. There's only one you!

In stillness we not only find physical wellbeing but also connect to our soul. From this place we can discern, without outside influence, what are our values, our gifts, and choose our purpose in life.

What are values?

Values reflect in the way we behave. This is what other people see of us and we therefore create in the world. The question here is not to discuss moral values in terms of who is doing things the right or the wrong way, but rather, to discover what is important to you. In our busy societies it is easy to forget our true values and be influenced by what others or society insists is important. When we are not acting in accordance with our own values we feel internal conflicts. We are neither at peace, nor being authentic. It leads to half-hearted actions and potentially animosity eventually towards those whom we believe are preventing us from being ourselves. If we are not living by our values then we are also therefore not looking after ourselves. Your values are so important that they should form the core of your lifestyle, making time to ensure they are expressed.

To start, let's think about what's important to you. You could note some of the answers to these questions in your journal.

If we take a moment to look at the things that are close to us :

- what we would like to spend hours doing and for which we wouldn't need to be paid!
- What objects do you always have close to you? Why?
- Outside of basic living expenses, what do you spend your money on?
- If the world was about to end, how would you spend your final hour?

Are there any common themes within your answers? Note them down. They could be activities, ways of being e.g. being charitable, reading, spending time with close friends or family. John Demartini's *Values Factor* or an interesting book to learn more.

Sometimes when we have been investing a lot of time caring for other people and activities which don't nourish our own values then this exercise can be difficult at first. Take your time. You can also try these two approaches to :

- Think back to the moments when you were freer. Let yourself daydream about what you enjoyed doing as a child. Does remembering a particular activity, place or memory spark any excitement? Follow that feeling and note the ideas of what you enjoyed.
- Try to find at least half an hour at the weekend to rediscover your spontaneity. Don't plan anything in advance, simply decide just before or let yourself wander. Where do you find yourself heading? What activities or objects catch your attention? Note these down.

When we have an idea of the activities and ways of being that are important to us, we can think about how to ensure there is space in our lives from them. Doing things we enjoy and in line with our values gives us energy. Doing things which go against our values or that we believe don't align with our notions of well-being zap our energy and very quickly. This is where we are living by other's expectations (or what we believe their expectations to be, because sometimes we're not even sure if we're honest) and therefore their values instead of our own. Over the long-term this can lead to burn-out or feelings of anaesthesia as we constantly force ourselves, ultimately forgetting who we are. Our social environment has many expectations of us and we also place enormous burdens on ourselves. It's a very common occurrence for people to forget their values or indeed to have never taken the time to think about what's important to them and therefore *consciously* make space in their lives for the important things. Knowing your values helps you to prioritize where you are spending your time and energy. Combining this knowledge with some simple time management tools we can finally make time for what or who is important to us, including most importantly ourselves! Empowerment comes from being conscious of how we use our time, in the same way as when we are conscious of everything in our lives. Awareness is the first step in the ability to make different choices so we can live more enriched lives.

Our values really show us what is important to us in terms of how we prioritize our actions. This is why culturally, an organization's values can be seen as a supra-set of the behaviours of the people that interact there. How is the organisation spending it's time? What actions can we see? Where are we losing time on things that we don't value, that are just draining people's energy? How can we prioritise what is important? The collective well-being comes then from the ability of the individuals that comprise the organization to work in alignment with their intrinsic motivations. We then find purpose in our actions.

Being Before Doing

Having found a sense of calm and space for ourselves as part of our Mindfulness practice, we're better positioned to start being clear about what our intention or personal statement is going to be. Intention is key. Like a compass it provides the direction. Integrating a Mindfulness practice into our lives could be compared to allowing the compass dials to settle before we set off in any particular direction. Intention meanwhile is like asking ourselves where we want to go? Imagine trying to set off on your journey before setting the destination. Difficult to be confident about actually getting to our intended destination, unless of course we don't mind and then we can simply enjoy the journey and let life decide! We'll talk about surrender later.

Intention is knowing at any moment why I'm doing or saying something. What am I trying to achieve through this action? In this conversation? If you don't know, then don't do it! It sounds like you might be wasting your energy. Question any actions that you are taking which feel like they are on autopilot. On the contrary, when we commit to a direction our actions become more deliberate. We've given purpose to what we do.

"Act as if what you do makes a difference. It does."
William James

When looking for intention, a helpful step is to delve deeper into understanding your essence. Who you are on a deeper level and in relation to the world. When we choose our intention we are essentially locking in what we wish to experience ourselves as *being* and consequently what we wish to see manifest in our lives.

The philosophy of Dharma talks about excellence in the beginning being optimal thinking, excellence in the middle as optimal choices and excellence in the end is optimal outcomes. Simon Haas wrote a wonderful book on this topic called *The Book of Dharma : Making Enlightened Choices*. In particular, he notes that *"our thoughts, words and actions spring from our state of being"*. If we choose to be peaceful then the chances are substantially higher that we think peaceful thoughts and therefore act in a peaceful manner towards others.

When we choose positive states of being, we are more conscious of how to differentiate the potential actions in our lives which Haas defines as *"the ability to distinguish between what uplifts us and what degrades us, what nurtures and what promotes the conditions of human flourishing and also what destroys those conditions both for ourselves and others."* Essentially, we see what thoughts, choices and courses of action are potentially good for us or not and we can consciously choose to *embody* those that uplift.

But how do we choose what to *be*? It's unusual to set goals in this way when we were taught to think about what we want to *do* or *own*. Also when thinking about ways of being there is so much choice! Would you like to be more loving? More active? Gain more clarity? More calm? Feel more secure? We then look at how we can incorporate that into our lives and the barriers that we are placing on ourselves to achieve that state, or the superfluous activities which are not taking us in that direction and therefore are not good for our well-being.

Exercise : What do I want to experience myself as being?

As part of a new emerging culture or society, what qualities do I want to share? In my day-to-day, what do I want to be more of?

> Affectionate, loving, intimate, gentle
> Stable, secure, grounded
> Active, energized, courageous, passionate
> Sensitive to my emotions and senses, joyous
> Clarity, self-confident, discerning, simplifying
> Curious, flexible, collaborative, open-minded
> Detached, balanced, independent, free
> Fluid, transparent, trusting, peaceful
> Receptive, present & listening, connecting
> Intuitive, aware, attentive
> Unifying, harmonising, coherent
> Spiritual, purposeful

1. Circle those that you feel are your strengths (so you would feel comfortable saying "*I am…*"). Feel free to add other qualities that come to mind, the list is not exhaustive.
2. Underline those qualities that you would like to integrate more of into your way of being. Feel free to add other qualities that come to mind but try to avoid qualities that are dependent on other's validation e.g. being funny as you may determine this by needing other people to laugh at your jokes. Try the objective of being light-hearted instead, humor can be part of that.
3. Think about and perhaps journal a few lines about why adopting that quality would help you. This will serve as your motivation. Be sure that your reasons for wanting to

integrate them align with your sense of self i.e. that these are qualities that you feel are an important part of you but that you are not demonstrating today, rather than to please someone else e.g. being 'nicer' or get to an external outcome e.g. secure a new job.

4. Choose one or two to work on and note down some small actions that you could carry out in order to demonstrate that quality and therefore experience yourself as being that quality. For example, if I wanted to be more courageous and I am introverted then I might choose to say hello to someone different each day. If I am extroverted then I might resolve to say what I believe in every circumstance in a kindly but authentic way. Only you can know the size of the step that is good for you. Don't try to make the changes too big to start with as it can be easy to demotivate when adjusting our behaviours. You can always increase the difficulty later as you gain confidence.

5. As you go about your day to day actions, ask yourself *"What would "courage" do in this moment? I will therefore...»* to help you to determine the best course of action for you. Be disciplined and consistent. If you deviate from that, try not to judge yourself as it won't help, simply notice it and choose another course of action. So if you find yourself thinking or doing something which is not in line with your desired outcome then simply look at it with curiosity telling yourself *"oh that's interesting that I reacted in that way... or that I chose to say that...., instead I choose.....".* This retrains the brain without falling into patterns of guilt.

This exercise is designed to place you directly in an action mode. I find that when we have the courage to step into new ways of being (and therefore behaviours) directly, we validate ourselves and through the reactions of others to our new behaviour. We get to the *"I am...."* in a direct rather than an indirect way.

As William James very poignantly said "*To change one's life : 1. Start immediately. 2. Do it flamboyantly. 3. No exceptions*". We need to be consistent in our actions, but we can be kind with ourselves in the process. If we persist we are quickly into the flow of experiencing ourselves as bigger and brighter in this new behaviour and it is often recognized by those around us, we receive their feedback and it becomes positively self-reinforcing. It is generally accepted that it takes at least 21 days to change a behavior. Embodyment has impacts on our whole way of life so it can take longer, but afterwards we feel confident that our thoughts, words and actions are congruent.

Keep in mind that changing behaviours can feel awkward because we have become so used to operating in particular ways, perhaps an entire lifetime! Changes can therefore surprise the people around us. When we see their surprise it can be unsettling but keep persisting. It's validation that your actions are concrete. I describe it sometimes like a child learning to stand. Its legs wobble, it falls but it keeps getting up because it knows inside that this is a natural thing for it to do, that it will succeed. Treat yourself kindly, self-judging is very damaging. In a similar way, surround yourself with people who will support your new behaviours and distance yourself from those who criticize. Positivity is key!

Once you have chosen a characteristic you can check your real motivations using a Five Whys exercise (see the example below). In this exercise we take a statement which would normally be a given and we ask ourselves why? We're questioning both our motivation and how we would see that way of being playing out in our lives. Note the first reply that comes into your head. Then ask why? again, noting the response and continue this process another three times. This is a way of clarifying your intention. When you see it written down it becomes more powerful too. You start to give form to your intention as part of our natural creative visioning process.

Example of the Five Whys exercise based on the statement : "I am loving"

Why? Because I take the time to listen to and connect with the people I meet

Why? Because I am interested in knowing who they truly are

Why? Because I'm curious and because I feel deep listening is important

Why? Because it's one of the greatest gifts we can offer to another person

Why? Because we are often so busy that we don't take the time to listen to one another. Being heard is a key need.

So in particular, I will choose to be loving by adopting a behaviour of slowing down and listening deeply to people because this is what I value. Does it feel right now that you can see it questioned like this? If not choose a different way of being and redo the exercise.

Choosing a way of being as a starting point can help us to clarify which actions are subsequently important to us, or the activities that we'd like to become involved in so that we can discover these qualities of ourselves. It puts us on a path of being more deeply in harmony with our true desires. The answers we get from the Five Whys may not be what we initially thought was our reason for engaging in an activity, particularly if we have been operating on autopilot. For example, I may discover that I was trying to be loving by doing things for other people (because perhaps I thought that this was important to them), whereas actually I'd like to be a better listener. This aligns better with my sense of what it means to be loving.

As we learn to trust our intuition, the need to question in this way is replaced by a simple sense of knowing what feels right. But even until we get to that stage, when we set out on a particular path we can be open to the feedback that life gives to us. If doors keep closing then don't force, just listen and observe where life is encouraging you to keep growing. Are you seeing opportunities to demonstrate your new behaviour, to be courageous or loving for example. Is it giving you energy and helping you to feel good about yourself, irrespective of what others may say about what is right for you?

Believing that you are *not* a particular quality or way of being can also block that from your life. But we can reintegrate it by changing our belief. This is why calming our inner critics and positive psychology are important. Rather, keep in mind your intention for the day, for the activity you have planned or to honor how you feel at any moment.

At this stage, we have started to determine what is important to us and set our intention to experience ourselves in a particular way. Our choices and actions are a natural consequence of that.

Choices are essentially made from a place of love or fear (by love we mean self-love and love of others generally). Fears such as rejection or humiliation can lead to us to take actions which are not right for us but based on pleasing others or some other external factor. Acting in a particular way in order to fit in, i.e. to belong somewhere, would be a good example. It's not wrong to feel the need to belong as human beings are essentially communal, it just needs to be the right group for you based on your true needs and desires. It should *feel* right for you, not stressful. This is directing our choices and actions from a place of self-love.

When we are being mindful we develop more clarity and can therefore look at our intention in anything we do. Does this choice or action align with how I want to be? What is my intention in this job? Is it helping me to be peaceful, or loving for example or is there an adjustment which needs to be made to allow that? What is my intention in this relationship? In this conversation or even argument? This perspective gives us the power to change direction in anything which is not in line with what we want to be in the world. We can essentially lead ourselves with more integrity and conviction.

Tuning Into Our Emotions

It is actually very important to master listening to and then surrendering our emotions as part of self-leadership. This is not only so that they can support our inner compass but also so that they do not pollute our thinking. When we gain more emotional balance, our choices tend to support our well-being and to be more compassionate towards others. We are not driven by our emotional reactions, but rather we can listen to them in order to make choices which feel right to us.

We experience emotional build-up if we are not listening to and acting on the signals that our emotions are trying to provide to us. The consequence is that we develop thoughts and patterns of behavior which are most probably reactional. Gray-LaViolette's 1981 research which links psychology and neurophysiology shows us that feeling tones organize thoughts into our memory banks according to their varying degrees. On this basis, if we decide to let go of a feeling, we essentially allow all of the associated thoughts (or 'stories' that we invent to self-validate a particular reaction) to dissipate. We are not triggered in the same way in future. It comes back to the old adage *"what got you here won't get you there"*. Indeed our old emotional reactions developed in our early years, often don't serve us as adults. Have you ever seen an adult throw a tantrum in the middle of a meeting? Point made. We all have these triggers, but whether we keep them or not is a choice.

As we listen initially, we may notice that some feelings stay longer than others. When a feeling stays with us for more than 3 minutes then it is worth looking into what it has triggered within us. Since we repeat patterns (which we can call *strategies* for solving the event we are faced with), they most likely come from a much earlier event when we were faced with an issue that we had no strategy for solving. When we have no strategy, then the moment in question can generate a trauma (which does not necessarily infer that it is a major trauma) at which point we store a belief and create a strategy for future use. It is these strategies which become our automatic reactions. This is a perfectly natural process. They protect us. The problem is that these strategies may support us in one phase of our lives but no longer be useful in our current context where perhaps as an adult we don't need to be as fearful.

When we first start to listen to what our bodies are trying to tell us it can be hard. We're often taught to do the exact opposite and pretend everything is ok, that emotions are unwelcome, especially in corporate environments, or if our upbringing made it unacceptable to express them. We suppress them also because we're afraid that they will overwhelm us. They have been denied for so long that we can physically feel that build-up and with it a lot of fear in releasing it.

When identifying an emotion, naming it correctly will often make us feel just a little lighter, or perhaps we might sigh, relax a little. Its like acknowledgement that we've been heard. Since emotions are our body's way of communicating with us, it is exactly what just happened! You have just given yourself some empathy.

Exercise in expressing what I felt in my body:

- Lie down in a quiet place where you won't be disturbed for five minutes. Relax each part of your body slowly, by placing your attention on one area after the other saying in your mind, I relax my forehead, I relax my eyes… (you can use a body scan recording for this to help initially, although these generally take longer than five minutes so allow extra time). Then simply listen to your breath for a moment.

- As you lay there, how are you feeling? Agitated? Tense? Peaceful? Try not to judge the feeling, just let it be. What might your body be trying to tell you through that feeling? Are you feeling fearful? Angry? Serene? Where in your body can you feel this? In a tense neck? Or a knotted stomach? Or are you calm? How might you adjust your posture to relax a little further? What might your feelings or your body be telling you so that you can improve your circumstances?

Our emotions are important signals, they guide us through life. If we have been suppressing them for some time, however, they can sometimes seem extremely powerful or to the contrary we don't feel them at all. We use all kinds of diversions in order to avoid listening to them for fear of being overwhelmed by those that have been particularly suppressed. There can be fear around letting them out. They are never bigger than us no matter what we might think. Acknowledge the validity of that fear since it is your reality and breath through it, only then will you get to the underlying emotion that needs to be cleared.

When we feel an emotion and let it pass, we know that it is not stronger or bigger than we are and this in turn builds a strong sense of self. We can ask ourselves, ok so I felt angry and so what? When it has passed we can look more calmly at the situation. What are the facts of the event, and therefore what would I like to do about it? Letting ourselves feel an emotion diffuses it and is much healthier for our bodies as they don't cumulate. If we let them build up then they become like a barrel full to the brim which eventually overflows, usually at the wrong moment as we overreact to a much less consequential event. The more we incorporate this practice of letting them diffuse into our daily lives, the less impactful the emotion. They dissipate quickly and we become more distanced from some of the more trivial issues that we encounter during our day. We gain a sense of emotional balance which we can compare to a reed in a lake which at first may move abruptly when the wind blows, but as time goes by and it strengthens it sways less and less until it sways only slightly in the face of an event. We are not blown off our center, despite the fact that the emotion is felt.

It can be useful to keep a diary of your emotions to see how frequently they occur and be aware of when/where they happen. With this information it can be easier to notice patterns and identify how we can satisfy our needs in order to be in a more peaceful state.

There are many techniques available for addressing old emotions and reversing the associated outdated beliefs in order to gain more emotional balance. One such technique is Emotional Freedom Technique (EFT) but there are many which encourage us to work through the body directly.

What is Emotional Freedom Technique?

EFT is a tapping technique that encourages energy to circulate within the body through the meridians. It works on the acupressure points of the body. When energy is 'blocked' we can feel low and sluggish, perhaps even depressed and our thoughts about ourselves tend to be more on the negative side. When it is circulating at its highest we feel love and joy. No need to analyse the why it is there in the first place in detail, we just 'unblock' it.

Meridian based therapies were based on the work of John Diamond an Australian psychiatrist and kinesiologue. In 1970 he introduced the idea of touching acupressure points whilst making positive affirmations in order to address emotionally based problems. In the early eighties his work was deepened by Roger Callahan who first used tapping on these points and using more precision around the emotional issue (Thought Field Therapy). Then Gary Craig who attended Callahan's training in the early 1990s once again evolved it into Emotional Freedom Technique (EFT) and made the approach available to everyone through the internet. Many videos can be found today to support your own practice which makes it an empowering self-help technique, although there are also many qualified practitioners around.

During an EFT session, we identify with a particular situation that we perceive as negative. When we think of it, it's likely to have associated feelings. We ask where you can feel it in your body or the energy field around you? If the person can describe the feeling by associating it with colors, or density, or size and shape? Does it look or feel like an object e.g. a heavy weight or a mud puddle? We try not to rationalize what is felt, just trust the first things that comes to mind. We then listen into what the feeling is telling us. Perhaps hopelessness in the form of a belief such as *"I'm never going to be able to complete this assignment"*.

There is then a sequence in which the meridians are tapped in order to start circulating our energy whilst repeating the negative phrase. As we do so, we find that we feel a little better and the initial belief starts to feel inappropriate, it shifts to a slightly more positive perspective. In the example provided this might mean *"This assignment is going to be difficult"*. Continuing on with the tapping this might become *"I can do it if I have help"* and eventually *"I can do it, I know how to start"*. We often feel lighter and more empowered. As we subsequently move into action we experience the belief as erroneous because the emotion does not submerge us anymore with big alarm bells.

One of the first things that EFT helped me with was a feeling of claustrophobia I'd had for a long time. I certainly couldn't remember what caused it. I experienced feelings of panic that surfaced when I found myself in an enclosed space, but in particular where I couldn't move my arms. During the session, not only did the emotion lift little by little but I saw a particular image which surprised me. There I was, at the age of what must have been around six years old. I was playing at my best friend's house and she and her sister had decided to wrap me in a quilt, to sit on me and tickle me! Quite an innocent, playful moment but I had felt so stuck and helpless in that quilt as they refused to stop that I had panicked and told myself "never again will I let myself be trapped like that". Don't worry about getting to the actual exact belief or even needing to see exactly where the emotional trigger comes from, or understand why. We simply diffuse the underlying emotion. In tapping I also realized that I felt a sense of betrayal by my friend for not releasing me from my captivity, but rather listening to her sister's encouragements to continue. That was even more of a discovery for me so I tapped on that too! It's always interesting to see how our inner dialogue evolves as we continue tapping, how our strategies of protection are inter-related. A month or so later I found myself stuck in an elevator in a New York hotel for a good thirty minutes and managed to stay perfectly calm! Life just loves to check if we've validated and integrated what we've learnt, just to show us how we've progressed. Don't forget to recognize your progress. It's very nourishing to know that our efforts are working. It's rarely a quick path so this positive reinforcement is vital to sustaining our motivation in more difficult moments.

The point here is not to detail the EFT process fully, there are many books available on the subject, but to show how the mind and emotions are interlinked. What I love about EFT, even though it can seem a little strange to tap, is that it avoids us getting stuck in our stories in continuing to identify with them. The *why* doesn't matter, only clearing the residue of emotions from the trauma and therefore releasing the beliefs.

I also like the humanistic approach to addressing our difficulties which relates our behaviours to an energetic scale of well-being. It suggests that when we find our energy levels at the lower end of the scale, because we are playing out patterns in our minds that we don't know how to escape or we believe are serving us, then we are all capable of states such as violence and depression. This means that we are all innately have the possibility to move up the scale too in order to experience states of joy, peace and love more regularly in our lives.

These techniques can be useful for overcoming many emotional issues and removing barriers that we place on ourselves. At higher energy levels it is far more difficult to feel bad about yourself. Have you ever seen how radiant someone looks when they're in love and they feel on top of the world? But we often look for that same feeling of love on the outside of ourselves through addictions, needy behaviour or projecting on others. In these cases the feeling doesn't last or live up to our expectations. This is why loving oneself is primary.

Note that energy shifts can make us feel tired so try to ensure you give yourself some space and time to rest if you try these techniques. It's just your body readjusting to the release of old emotional energy that it no longer needs. You are rebalancing and literally repairing through a parasympathetic state because the body detects that it no longer needs to be in a state of fight-flight with respect to the trauma that has been resolved.

In his book *"Letting Go : The Pathway to Surrender"*, David R. Hawkins also recommends an alternative to EFT which is simply to surrender the feeling. We recognize it, feel it and then give it up to something bigger than ourselves (be that God, the divine, the Earth, or just simply drop it) trusting that we don't need it anymore. It has done it's job in communicating to us, no need to hang on to it.

As I was investigating emotional balance, I also learned that the Five Animals sequences of Qi Gong represent different emotions : the Tiger for moving anger (from the liver and gall bladder); the Deer for moving fear (from the kidneys); the Monkey for circulating joy (through the heart and small intestine); the Bear for transforming worry into serenity (by working on the spleen); and the Crane for sadness (the lungs and large intestine). So as we are working on these movements the energies are rebalancing in our systems at the same time.

For some behavioural patterns there can be unconscious beliefs that are blind spots to us, and until we un-knot them they drive us. I have found that kinesiology is also very useful here. These beliefs get interlinked and our minds are wonderful at trying to hide them from us!

When we put a little effort into cleaning up some of the old emotions and beliefs that are no longer serving us then we give ourselves the possibility of removing barriers that might be regularly tripping us up. What we resist persists so when we become willing to feel and release the emotion, it dissipates. Life somehow seems less heavy or complicated. It is our perspective of, or belief about a situation that makes it difficult, not the situation itself. When we listen to or diffuse the emotion, we can look at the facts more objectively and see ways forward.

Listening to our emotions and our intuition are great compasses in life. To self-realise it is also important to ensure we are nourishing our self-esteem in a positive way.

Bling From Within

Very often we hear that bling is vulgar, or passé, then the next day that it's fun and glamorous. The critics don't seem to be able to decide! The funny thing is that if we asked anyone whether it would be a good or bad thing to shine like a diamond from the inside, there's highly likely to be unanimity, "Bring it on!". Self-care is a huge topic, we could dedicate an entire book just to this. For the purposes of self-leadership we are not so much interested in the external aspects, but to relook our insides so they are just as beautiful as our outsides!

Radiating positive energy from the inside is captivating. But the question is how do you do it? I'd simply like to start by saying that nothing is more infectious and beautiful to another receptive human being than a genuine smile and that sparkle that appears in the eyes of those connected to spirit and a sense of joy.

According to a recent Chinese study of what makes us attractive or not to others (from 2014 by Yan Zhang, Fanchang Kong, Yanli Zhong & Hui Kou) found that being seen as decent or honest made a big difference. What we perceive as decent or honest may vary, but clearly our way of being with others counts for a lot. Smiling, kindness and joy are never out of style, so give them a special place in your life! This way of being will not only make you feel more positive but this is the energy that you will then bring to the environment around you.

Not only do you feel better when you are kinder to yourself, when in particular we learn to curb those critical thoughts, but it can be seen on the outside, whether reflected in facial expressions, posture and general radiance. Over and above the physiological impact, we develop our spirituality when we are not devoting energy to negative outlets such as self-criticism and the drama outside. How are you taking a moment to nourish yourself every day?

Here's a summary of five ways you can develop self-care by cultivating your inner garden:

- **Being present with yourself** by listening to both your body and your emotions
- **By daring to take time for yourself**, even if others judge (physically allocating time to your body - you have the body that you have but the more you love it and treat it well the better it will of course respond. This seems obvious but sometimes we can be our own worst enemies!). Do activities that you enjoy. Listen to your limits, especially when you find yourself giving in too much to others. Gain clarity and separate from your life what enhances it from what detracts from it – remove anything which is not in line with your values and your highest potential.
- **Cultivate connection with others** which we can do through self-expression, honesty and developing assertiveness :
  - Express who and what you choose to share with the world without aggressiveness or judgement
  - Develop active listening skills through empathy and respect
  - Express gratitude (which can take time to feel if either you have been through a traumatic period or you have never learnt to connect to your emotions so be patient with yourself)
- **Align your life-style with who you are** using auto-empathy and by moving towards your dreams
- **Discipline your mind** by letting go of judgements and transforming them into an understanding of and a satisfaction of your needs. Change "*what I hold against you is….*" to "*what I aspire to is….*". Learn to tune into and savour the beauty of each moment of life.

If the last suggestion seems too far-fetched to you then I invite you to keep practicing Mindfulness. With persistence you will likely get to this state, finding that your heart fills up and your sense of connection is more fulfilled. So I won't dwell on that here, just a friendly reminder to practice, practice, practice! It's like riding a bike.

You can also create your own bubble where you can take time out (especially if you live with others), perhaps in a favourite quiet space where you can regenerate. A lot of people do this in nature. Why? Because reconnecting with nature provides us with a sense of balance and replugs us back into what is essentially the bigger picture and a vast energetic grid. This grid surrounds us at all times but in nature it is less polluted with negative energy vibrations than in more densely populated areas. Everything living has an electromagnetic field of energy around it. It's your linkage between your internal and external world. In their book "Presence: Exploring Profound Change in People, Organizations, and Society", Senge, Scharmer, Jaworski and Flowers describe in some very moving accounts, the life-changing shift in understanding that we can benefit from when we truly reconnect to nature and feel our place within that.

We will not refer to any particular religion, but whether you refer to this source energy as the infinite, God, or the divine, there is a field of consciousness and energy freely available to us to tap into and ensure we're literally blinging at any moment we choose.

Through self-leadership, your soul is just waiting to guide you to fill up with the feelings of love, peace and joy, whilst also revealing your majesty to you. It's a process of simply rediscovering the fact that you are amazing, but in our busy day-to-day it doesn't seem so easy to remember. Because of that it's important to take time out to ensure our energy is remaining positive and literally flowing by taking time to reconnect to the stillness of our inner and outer worlds.

Unconsciously we all give out signals and like emotional intelligence, we can work on improving them. In fact the better we feel, the more positive these signals become automatically. People can sense the density of this field as it carries the weight of much of our emotional history. Like a big log book, it helps guide us through life holding different layers of understanding in energetic form. You can feel when you walk into a room where there has been an argument, it feels heavy. Or can you tell when someone comes up too close behind you without having to turn your head? And you've heard the expression moving out of your comfort zone? Words are not chosen by chance, there is literally a zone and energy which is more or less dense around you.

We can literally wake ourselves up through the correct use of our energy, in particular by avoiding negativity in our speech and close environment. Be careful of the slogans and words you use. They are very powerful in their impact on how we feel. Our behaviour and our energy is also influenced by the five people closest to us so ensure to keep your relationships and dialogue positive. Distance yourself from people, media or blogs that repeatedly criticize others (this is a way of proning non-violence to others).

Creating a supportive, nurturing environment is a lifestyle choice. A positive self-esteem means knowing what it is important to distance from our lives so that we can function in a way which allows us to maintain our well-being and align with our values. You are responsible for your joy. We always have a choice and if you make one and don't like the outcome then simply choose again.

Contrast

I feel very deeply as a guiding principle that leadership is within everyone. We need different characteristics to take the lead in guiding situations according to the context. Sometimes the driver might be humour, sometimes authority, sometimes the ability to encourage dialogue. We can either find these in ourselves or partner with others who may be better at sharing them than us. That's where great teams flourish, when they can respect each other's strengths so that almost like in cycling, they naturally let the right person lead according to the context so that the others benefit from their ability to manoeuvre a particular phase, tiring as little as possible. They know that another person will take over when the context changes. When we're confident of our gifts we allow others the possibility to demonstrate theirs too without the need to compete in the traditional negative sense of the word.

So when would I take the lead? In terms of finding one's leadership strengths, I've come to believe that the notion of finding and understanding the contrast in one's life is particularly important.

Our contrasts are the themes that run through many of the events in our lives. They can often be determined through the moments that we feel deeply hurt us, or we feel uncomfortable in ourselves about. We don't always take sufficient time to stand back and gain perspective on what these events have brought to us. We attach our identities to the difficulties of stories instead of the beauty. As we go through them and come out of the other side we discover something new about ourselves. I'm strong, or I am peaceful, or I am beautiful, or I am resilient despite all the odds that appeared to be against me. It's very much part of the process of experiencing who I chose to be. Life positions us so that we can receive confirmation of that. So I can get to the point of saying "*I am*". Looking back over the perhaps several instances of these events, if we can manage to take a helicopter view and see gratitude for how we've grown through the experiences and what we have discovered about ourselves then the circle is complete and we can be thankful to all those people involved in helping us to see our truth. We see the perfection in how it all unfolded. We can then take that into our day-to-day and share it with others as our gift with deep authenticity. Over and above the capabilities we develop technically, these amazing strengths are simply a part of who we are that sometimes we just don't even notice their force or we don't necessarily build on them. This is why I believe so strongly in sharing stories so we acknowledge the power behind them and why everyone, absolutely everyone, has a story to tell and a leadership strength to uncover.

So when we are choosing to be something or have a purpose in discovering ourselves to be much more than we ever imagined, understanding our life challenges offers us a way in. In other words, it can be helpful to experience what we are not in order to establish who we truly are. I might, for example, spend a long time being aggressive because I feel I need to defend myself in a hostile environment until I decide to be peaceful because it serves me better.

Contrast is quite the opposite of duality. It teaches us that there is no good and bad, but rather that in order to truly see something, we simply need another reference point. On this basis we often label the reference as being negative until we understand what it is allowing us to discover about ourselves. I essentially see what I do not want to be in order that I can *choose* differently. It is free will without judgement. Everything is part of a scale of states of being which we choose to experience.

Here are some questions that you can ask yourself to find your contrast :

1. Think about the place that you live in, the environment that you work in or the family that you are a part of. How do you see yourself as being different or a contrast to that? I don't believe that we find ourselves in certain environments by accident. In what ways do you criticize these because they don't correspond to your view of how the world should be?

How does it feel unjust or awkward? What story do you tell yourself about that situation in order to feel like you are doing things right where others may not be? This can help us to discover self-reinforcing beliefs that are keeping us stuck in a particular story, or in separation from others. As we develop a more objective view of the circumstances and look at the positive in what we have gained from growing and distancing ourselves from the story we can get to the thank you. For example, out of my experience of harassment, I may emerge with a sense of forgiveness or realizing my strength and ability to look after my needs.

2. Think back to a difficult phase of your life, did you change your behaviour subsequently? What did you discover about yourself? Perhaps how much resilience you had? Or how compassionate you can be? That newly discovered characteristic will be a force for you to build on in your life and a key strength to contribute to a group. It is always our perspective of a situation and how we choose to live through it that leads us to growth or not. It is important of course to distance ourselves from anything which is not beneficial to our well-being but in doing so we can see it as just a reference when the hurt and emotion is diffused from the story.

To illustrate the first point, as part of my journey I delved into a recurring history of separation in my life. This was not only because of the obvious personal events such as being a child from a divorced family, living several magical but long-distance relationships and then my divorce, but the interesting part was how I was unknowingly reinforcing that. Since that first separation as a child, where I initially gave my power away, I had been telling myself that I needed to battle through life and that was my idea of the leadership I needed to demonstrate in order to move myself out of that space. That all my reasons for having a successful career and everything I wanted in life were due to a hard-working, not needing or asking for help, independent nature. This coupled with early management roles were creating subconscious barriers between me and other people, perhaps to keep them at a distance. Sure I was friendly and caring but underneath it I felt the separation that I was imposing on myself all over the place. All of the strategies I had built for reacting to life's stresses and challenges were built around the idea that these behaviours were helping me to succeed. Quite the opposite, I wasn't truly being vulnerable and letting people in. I was stuck in my story of how this distance was ok and I could live with it until the day came where I had to admit it wasn't working for me anymore.

What is also fascinating are the similarities in contrast that can exist between generations. Beliefs and traumas can be transmitted down the family line as the latest research in epigenetics is showing us. In my particular case, one side of my family is dispersed all over the world and I recently discovered that both great grand-parents on that side were orphans. People play out the themes in different ways in their own lives, but it is interesting to see how we can sometimes be affected by patterns in our subconscious that we don't even know how we created in the first place! We simply need to look at them objectively to review how perhaps we are still reinforcing what we don't want instead of what we do.

As it happens, I'm excellent at making linkages between ideas and people, connecting. The more I developed my ability to connect on a deeper level, the more profound my findings and relationships felt to me and the deeper the impact it seemed to have on the people around me in terms of supporting them. Working through these separation issues helped me to really connect to my love of humanity and how indeed we can develop different ways of connecting between us, making better choices without blame or shame.

A friend recently told me she saw an image of Papa Smurf when she was thinking of something for me. This of course made me giggle, but thinking about it more deeply, it's perhaps not so far from the truth. The idea of being a Mama Smurf who supports a whole village of wonderfully diverse smurfs to find and use their talents, being present and always there to serve in order to ensure harmony reigns. Diversity within unity. Yes that sounds like me. Helping people connect to the beauty of their stories and their uniqueness is indeed something that moves me profoundly. I haven't turned blue yet, but who knows?

So we can take a different and more empowering view of our current (or past) situations if we ask ourselves how much of our circumstances are not by chance. What if we allowed ourselves to be the hero of our own story? We love to see other people do this in films and books but I believe that we all have this theme running through our lives if we look carefully enough and give ourselves the permission to recognize our amazing gifts. Again seeing the hero outside is disempowering. They have nothing more magical than you do. All of our stories require us to overcome adversity and set-backs in the same way in order to ultimately discover our magnificence. What if I am a calm, loving person who finds themselves in an environment of chaos or continually attracting conflictual people? Could this be in order to truly experience myself as peaceful? To live and experience what it means to be peaceful? To strive to bring peace to those around me as an example because it becomes so important to me. This is the gift that I share. When we are aware of it as a force and are living in alignment with that, it is extremely powerful and nourishing to our vital energy because we value ourselves and see our true magnificence. It is all there in order for us to experience and share our true nature.

Try sharing your stories with people around you. Talking through them with someone else can help you towards an authentic acceptance of your current perspective and therefore what the reality of those events might be helping you to experience that is positive. You may also find that your story resonates closely with the person with whom you share it. Voicing our stories is both healing to ourselves and can mirror the events that others have been living through too. It can take an instant to make the 180° pivot to step back from our stories and see the positive, the gift. So what is your story?

The more people share their stories honestly, the more we will collectively be able to become more accepting of ourselves and others. There will simply be no need to hide. Our stories are what brought us here today and when we don't judge them or those of others then we can collectively meet each other on another level. One that realizes that they are just stories and that on the other side of them is just love. I find these stories beautiful when they go full circle. I will always remember when someone said to me "*if it doesn't feel positive yet then you haven't got to the end of the story, keep going, keep looking for the thank you!*". At the time I was still hurting and attached to my story, but it kept me optimistic. If we keep putting one foot in front of another we get there eventually.

Here is an example of a story which links a person's understanding of their values and how life helped her to discover more of her essence and the perfection of non-duality :

I once met a Japanese lady who wanted to become a chef and so decided that she would move to London and then Paris in order to attend some of the most prestigious cooking schools. She wanted to combine this passion with her other passion for travelling. She was thoroughly enjoying herself until she received a message to say that her mother was ill back home in Japan and that she was to return home to look after her. Despite being concerned for her mother's welfare she returned home begrudgingly. She lived in a small, rural village where there was none of the diverse, stimulating international lifestyle that she'd found in the cosmopolitan cities that she'd become accustomed to and she imagined herself wasting away during the months that she watched over her mother's recovery. In the quiet of her day-to-day life she started to converse with the local artisans and discovered their stories through their stories and products. How much care and attention they put into their work. She learnt of the traditions in using some of the local ingredients and recipes that were becoming lost to the younger generation who don't cook so much. Given her ability to discern products from both her passion and her training, she realized how right under her nose there had been such a richness that she had ignored. She went full circle into feeling a state of pride for her heritage instead of feeling ashamed of it and on this basis decided to both teach people how to cook traditional recipes in her local community and also to travel the world in order to share her passion for these traditions and local producers by offering cooking classes. At the end of one such cookery workshops with her, not only had I discovered a whole world of ingredients that I had never used but she also presented us with a gift of a small sachet of green tea which had been produced in the vicinity of her home, delicately wrapped in a beautiful, handmade paper envelope as only the Japanese do! Drinking that tea afterwards reconnected me to the beauty of her story and a warm feeling of gratitude that it had made its way into my life.

Here she chose her purpose to be in sharing this understanding, her heritage and her cookery gift with others. She could have stayed stuck in a story of resentment but she chose to look for the positive. In doing so, it provided a motor for sharing who she is with the world. Often we seem to look for our purpose outside of ourselves when in fact it is a direction that we *choose* to invest our gifts in because we start to understand who we are in our essence.

A common theme in a lot of our lives, whether in family or corporate environments is the Karpman Drama Triangle of victim, aggressor and rescuer. Three people in regular conflict because of the rigid perspective that they take of their relationship to the others. It is a vicious circle which can repeat itself, but often the way it plays out in our life is to allow us to change positions. If we think back with humility to the different conflictual situations that we have found ourselves in we can at some point notice that we have likely been in each position. This is the balance that life brings to our perspective so that we can be in a place of non-judgement of others. This takes humility because often these positions pull us into postures of righteousness, so convinced that we are right and justified in our behaviour. The drama intensifies and we become stuck in our stories. Taking a step back to take stock of our current reality that we have become stuck in this vicious circle provides us with the choice to disengage, to change our circumstances and our beliefs about the situation of what is just or unjust for example. We choose to release the drama in our lives to move into a place of non-duality and inner peace.

Understanding this contrast and what it is helping us to learn is very powerful. Through it we see how we can get caught up in the fear and drama of our stories and those of others, so much so that it can be very, very addictive. If we do a 180° on those situations to look for the positive then we can see that there is so much more to the situation than we first imagined, or that we were clinging onto one outdated view of being right, or of what was possible for example. We see a different perspective on the other side as we let go of the drama by choosing to see the blessing. This drama is always presenting us with a reference point from which we can choose to experience ourselves differently. To release our old sense of self to become a much greater version. The free will to choose to move on. There can instead be a similar addiction in the peace that we find in that place on the other side of a drama which is far more rewarding for our well-being. Peace is a choice that everyone can make by letting go of the negative stories in our lives. This doesn't mean disengaging from life itself to become passive. On the contrary we make different choices which are more consciously beneficial to our well-being and to that of the collective.

Bear in mind that these themes tend to reoccur. Not necessarily in as dramatic a way each time if we are learning from them. We can compare this process of reliving the same theme as living in a spiral mode. We often believe that our paths unfold in linear way when in fact we recreate the same scenarios in order to see them either from the perspective of another person, or to look at them more and more finely. We could imagine growing in a sort of spiral that ascends. We see something different in a new perspective each time we get to the thank you or choose not to engage and identify so dramatically with the story. So this is a reminder not to ever be disheartened if you think you have healed a theme and it resurfaces. We can remember our amazing resilience and the gifts we learned from the last time a similar situation occurred. When we take that experience and do something constructive with it, including even just sharing our stories, I believe that at that point we become an inspiration and a support to others. This is how I like to imagine interdependent servant leadership, each person with this understanding of their gifts of humour, or resilience, or peace, or compassion, or strength offering that to create something bigger than one individual could.

I leave you with a quote from William James "*The greatest discovery of any generation is that a human can alter his life by altering his attitude*". Questioning our perspective allows us the freedom of discovering a deeper aspect of our true self and how this can propel us forwards to share our amazing gifts with the world.

Transformation : Creating movement towards the new

Let's investigate the motivation that I might need to delve into in order to change something about myself.

In order to want to re-create something for ourselves and particularly transform our environments, we quite often need to be in a state of discomfort. This provides us with the contrast that we discussed earlier. To look at the reality of the fact that something really isn't working for us and take a decision on that basis to change it, to rediscover and stand in our truth. Since most people don't like change, this can be particularly difficult and why organizational transformations rarely happen overnight but rather from solid, authentic honesty and commitment to implementing better choices.

So moving away from the quantitative indicators of what's wrong, although they can be particularly useful for facing realities, what personal factors do we have at our disposal to fuel this shift? Try anger. Yes, that emotion that gets banned from open expression at the corporate entrance, yet shows itself as endless complaining, blaming or the occasional outburst when things blow out of proportion.

Why do we always see anger as negative instead of the positive change agent that it can be? Perhaps because we're not great at listening to it or knowing what to do with it.

Aggression is anger's most basic form and is essentially a reaction because we feel there is no other way to engage with someone else in order to assert our needs. It's fear-based, controlling, and dominating as a means of achieving what is seen as the only solution. This is what many of us associate with anger and perhaps not the ideal way to channel it.

Venting is an alternative. Certainly its better to externalize than to keep anger inside, but it still keeps us in a place of victimisation in relation to the object of our displeasure, whether its a person or a system. And the person on the receiving end of the complaining still feels the intensity of the negativity of the situation, particularly if they are empathic. This is more of a coping mechanism until a similar event crops up again and we go back to complaining. Far more empowering is to learn to transform our anger into something new. A perspective, behaviour, a change of situation, it doesn't matter. Anger is a gift given to us in order to change the status quo, to propel us into action to improve what isn't right for us. This can be most constructive, not just for you but for the people around you too. Perhaps they were also dissatisfied with the object of your displeasure. Life is change. Without anger there would never have been movements to stop fur trading and the exploitation of children working in horrendous factory conditions. At the basis of anger is often a sense of injustice. Tune into that. Your anger speaks of what is unacceptable to you and to be in a place of self-leadership, using that energy to move into the new and transform your circumstances is key. Its believing you are capable of addressing this perceived imbalance and empowering yourself to follow through. It can be like rocket fuel when channelled well! Otherwise anger can ruminate and turn into bitterness or eventually explode in unfortunate circumstances.

Like any emotion, its how we listen to it and transform it that is key. Anger doesn't have to be against someone else. That's a pretty old-school way to look at things. Instead look at what you need to change in your part of a situation as you can't change someone else (for example, yelling at them is unlikely to bring about the result you're looking for, in fact quite the opposite as it makes them defensive). It's ok to be angry, especially when our boundaries have been crossed but its how we express our needs, the form that we give to that anger that matters. In any close relationship, insisting on being right or having the last word is never ideal in the long term. The alternative is not of course being a doormat or just overly kind for the sake of peace as that won't help either, resentment builds. It's about giving your needs a cleaner, more loving form of expression which is not hurtful and still respects the other. We always have a choice, which sometimes includes walking away if repeated occurrences of conflict are undermining us in some way. Tough love judges the behaviour not the person, who may not even be aware of their behaviour.

In terms of frustration with a system, decide what movement or group would you like to join in order to give an outlet to your desire for change? Surely there are others who feel the same way? What resources do you have around you to support you in making some changes? They don't need to be particularly big, just opportunities which allow us to move into action. List them and see which ones you can initiate today. Channel your frustration instead of sitting with it.

If we need to evacuate feelings of anger that are building then some of the traditional writing, art or pillow-hitting techniques can be pretty good for the short term! If the same situation keeps returning and we're feeling like déjà vu, that's when we need to move into action mode. The first step is to take an honest look at where our boundaries are being crossed or alternatively where the stance we are taking is perhaps too rigid, such that we feel attacked or our authority challenged by the other person. Write these down in order to externalize them, but then having done so we need to decide to take action or let the feeling go. Keep in mind that if we cling to the feeling then it will be difficult to shift. We have to want to be free of a feeling more than we want to keep it. This is why the discomfort needs to be so strong sometimes before we'll do anything. In "Letting Go : The Pathway of Surrender", David R. Hawkins says *"we think that somehow, if we hang onto that feeling, it is going to get us what we want"*. Ask yourself what is the benefit to me of keeping it? Are people protecting me? Does it help me feel righteous? Do I want to be the lesson-giver? Do I believe I can control the person's actions through my anger? These responses are intended to place ourselves in a superior or inferior role rather than meeting someone half-way. As Hawkins suggests *"We will almost always find that we have a fantasy that it will have some effect on the person and change their behaviour or attitude toward us. If we let go of that, we become willing to let go of the feeling"*.

During one of your journaling moments, list your dissatisfactions and your beliefs about them. How might you transform that negative belief into a new belief that could feel more beneficial? Then, how might you take baby steps to turning the situation around? It's very empowering to take that first step. This can involve accepting our feeling of pride or the the fact that it's easier to complain than to invest in changing. The importance is just to put ourselves into a place of action because otherwise suppressed anger becomes resentment. The important thing is to break the routine of who we think we are relative to that frustrating situation. Let the world see something different of you and let yourself experience that too. We can use our vital energy for greater benefit.

This section of the book has looked at how deep self-knowledge, self-acceptance and looking honestly at our current circumstances provides a basis for making more empowering choices for ourselves. It propels us into more proactive, compassionate self-leadership states and at this point we are in a much better position to wish to interact more harmoniously with others because we don't see their actions as necessarily limiting ours. We know and respect our own story.

Through our inner journeys we learn to accept ourselves as perfect as we are, all parts of ourselves. Despite that, however, when we see ourselves consciously, we also have the choice to evolve and reinvent ourselves, just because we can. Because we have that free will.

Because we limit ourselves in so many ways, when we are on a path to self-realization we can see the truth of how we do that with honesty, but we are also armed with the knowledge that we can transform that. There is inner peace and a discovery of our true potential on the other side of that journey. Why sit in discomfort or in a place of restriction when inner knowing offers us a better alternative?

COLLABORATE

With all the talk about increasing consciousness, we're heading towards a state of more healthy interdependency in our relations with others. We're becoming more aware that we are not islands but part of a whole global community. That our actions do indeed have an impact on others. That suggests we need the humility to take a deep look at our patterns of blaming, victimisation, co-dependency or isolation to move into modes of working more harmoniously through true, respectful partnership. This will essentially mean learning to be more open and authentic in our relations in order for these collaborations to be both nourishing and effective.

Egypt Calling

I'd like to share with you the insights I got from a visit to Egypt's Luxor region. During a recent visit, I was fortunate enough to spend a good amount of time meditating on the lush banks of the Nile so that my visits to the temples were well grounded to really feel into these sites. Extremely well versed in the use of consciousness as a way of life, the ancient Egyptians left us much wisdom.

As I was contemplating the hieroglyphics in the tomb of Tuthmosis III, I saw my life flash before me. So quickly that I could barely see the details, but I was left with the resounding gratitude of getting to this point of having re-centred my life around my consciousness practices and in doing so found God again and a state of inner peace.

As I meditated here, it felt to me that the region could represent many of the aspects of our divine feminine. It has a blissful, nurturing haze around it and an underlying deep mystic beauty that's just beckoning to be discovered. At this time in history where we rarely respect these feminine parts of our nature, it is interesting that there is much violence in contrast here. It could almost be a reflection of how we are treating these parts of ourselves. Indeed, I was again struck by the warm, nurturing, heart-centred hospitality through the people that I met during this trip and others that I have interacted with over many years.

Our feminine aspects (which are present in everyone) represent our intuition, our vulnerability, and creativity, in other words many of the parts of ourselves that we neglect, criticize, attempt to repress and therefore abuse. They raise immense amounts of fear in us because we have been taught that they are unacceptable, that we cannot trust them, or express them freely. To do so would make us weak or compromise our ability to succeed in life. It really depends on our definition of success and that's a choice, but certainly on a spiritual path the ability to welcome them with compassion and love is what brings us to wholeness. The same is true for our masculine parts also, I'm simply using the feminine as an example because it felt particularly important to me during this trip. I feel that also until many people get to the stage of welcoming all of those parts, our collective identities of masculine and feminine will always be biased. Each and every one of us have all of these aspects of masculine and feminine in differing qualities, we choose how to express them in our lives according to what we decide to be in any moment and therefore the actions we take. We were born with all of these aspects, perfect and whole, but sometimes we need to rediscover them by reintegrating them into our lives.

In spending time here with Egyptologist and meditation teacher Tracey Ash, she shared how we can learn from the story of Osiris and Isis, about the journey we go through during life in order to *piece ourselves back together* so to speak. A beautiful analogy that resonated a lot with me so I extrapolate here.

Osiris was a ruler of Egypt who was said to have lived by the order of *maat* which is the maintenance of natural order. Isis, the goddess of health, marriage and wisdom, was his consort and the sister of Set who represented violence and chaos. It is not established why, but history talks of Set murdering Osiris by cutting him into pieces which were spread across the provinces of Egypt, over which he subsequently imposed his rule. Isis's love drove her to find all of the pieces and reunite them so that Osiris could become whole again. In doing so she was granted the right to conceive a child, Horus. It was said that Horus was a vulnerable child who needed much protection initially from Isis. Eventually Horus grew up to defeat Set and replace him as the rightful ruler, once again maintaining order.

The fact of Isis searching far and wide for the pieces of Osiris was a deep act of love which we can understand from the traditional interpretation of what love means. From a spiritual perspective this story could also be likened to us deeply looking at and reintegrating all those parts of ourselves that we have ostracised by labelling them as not acceptable or as characteristics that don't make us worthy of love. When we exile like this, because of societal or family expectations, we essentially dismember ourselves. Everyone does this in differing ways and to differing degrees. This is why the story can be seen as so universal and why it is our own love and wisdom, like Isis', that enables us to put ourselves back together again.

That journey starts with inner peace and listening with love. Listening to ourselves is a true act of self-love and compassion. Starting this journey to genuine wholeness is not always easy. The important thing to remember is that we are already whole, it is just that we have suppressed parts of ourselves even if they might feel like they're missing, it's just because we've never discovered some of them. So let's start with moving away from the idea of duality, that there is necessarily right and wrong in how these parts of us should behave and whether they should or shouldn't exist. Already in doing so we soften our perception of ourselves and the outside world. I prefer to think that we use discernment in our day-to-day life since everything is choice, rather than judgement which has a harsh feel to it. As we become more compassionate, discover and accept these different aspects of ourselves, instead of fearing them, we also become more open to others. Having reintegrated them into our definition of self, we can also see and accept them in others. This is where we start to truly come together in a space which deeply respects diversity.

Judging Parts of Ourselves and Others

What do we mean exactly when we talk about judging ourselves? What does that behaviour look like?

- Putting ourselves down e.g. have you ever heard your inner critic telling you that you look overweight in a certain outfit? We can often be more harsh with ourselves than we are with others. If you listen carefully to your inner critic you may find that you would never dream of saying those things to someone else openly because you're aware of how hurtful they are. Our mind believes what we tell it regularly and propagates this knowledge to the rest of the body.
- Making ourselves feel guilty e.g. I should have known better, its all my fault. We are always learning in life. Dwelling on an incident is using precious energy and has a negative impact on our self-esteem. Apologise if it's appropriate and simply choose a different response next time. Yes you can!

If you feel you can't then I'd recommend going back to the section on EFT to drop that belief.

Wholeness as a way of being really encourages to put down as many of these judgemental thoughts as possible. The more mindful we are, the more aware we are which allow us the opportunity to reverse this toxic inner dialogue. If you catch yourself with a self-critical thought then simply pause, say to yourself that you choose again and replace it with a more kindly, reasonable statement.

Let's look now at how we may impose our judgement on others. Did you know that there is a crucial difference between the feelings of envy and jealousy?

To envy someone else is very natural. Its our inner motor telling us that we'd like to be or have what someone else has. Like the little brother or sister who wants to be able to do what their big brother or sister can do, like reaching the handle to open the door. It propels us to improve, it's a comparison which motivates. It's a question of possibility. We say to ourselves *"what if"*? It encourages us to try new things and reach higher to discover other aspects of ourself. Be curious about what it is that you envy in order to see some of the directions you'd like to go in and then imagine what actions you can put in place to achieve your own version of the wish that caused your envy.

Jealously meanwhile is destructive. It causes us to act in negative ways and is fuelled by the will to restrict, control or even damage another. The key here if you experience feelings of jealousy is to identify what freedoms you are not allowing yourself that the other person is. To reconnect to your own story and the possibilities you have to satisfy your needs rather than fixating on what others have that you want.

Competition can be the same. If fuelled by developing our own ideas, or by a healthy envy or admiration of others whose dreams tend in the same direction than ours then it is great for progressing both individually and together. Don't forget that we are not always facing a limitation which means we can all grow without restricting others. One person's win is not necessarily another's loss.

When competition is fuelled by control or a wish to destroy another then that's another matter. It puts us in a constant state of judgement and fear. All of our actions are fear-based. We're scared of moves and development that others achieve. We'll also spend much of our time and energy in a state of fear, calculating what their next move will be or how we can be better than them. It would be better to use that energy and visualisation positively, and to imagine our own possibilities.

So competition doesn't need to be based on a negative comparison with others. Imagine rather that envy could be a way of people all aspiring to bigger and brighter possibilities to reinvent themselves. We are not part of a zero sum game. We can all grow and achieve our dreams.

> *"There is a fine line between yes and no, good and bad are intertwined"*: Lao Tseu

Many aspects of life are polarities that are not separate one from another. We can look at them as data which allow us to move our lives in a direction we choose.

Choosing non-violence as a way of life

So let's get more practical. What are the ways that we can be "violent" with ourselves and others? It doesn't need to be physical and of course there are different degrees of violence. Some may surprise you...

To ourselves :

1. Judging ourselves
2. Not listening to our emotions or feelings, needs and desires
3. Being overly demanding of ourselves
4. Not expressing our joys, sadness or opinions
5. Getting angry with ourselves

To others :

1. By judging and criticising (e.g. you are so slow! You are good for nothing!)
2. By generalising (e.g. you are always late!)
3. By interpreting their behaviour also called projecting (e.g. when someone doesn't say hello to you, it must be because they don't like you)
4. Comparing people or trying to make them feel guilty (e.g. your exam results are awful, why didn't you work harder? Why can't you be like your sister?)
5. Labelling people according to your prejudices (e.g. all people who live on the street are incapable of fitting in)
6. Placing blame for circumstances on other people (e.g. its all your fault that I'm stuck in this job!) We always have choices in life and this reaction also gives our power to change our circumstances away.
7. Using threatening language or behaviour
8. Not listening to or even ignoring another person
9. Letting your anger take over your behaviour with others (e.g. shouting at someone instead of listening to your anger and using it to listen to what is wrong for you and make a request)
10. To give unsolicited advice

Take a moment to think about where you may have a tendency to use any of these behaviours. It is important to be honest with oneself in order to decide to change a behaviour. What we decide to turn a blind eye to will persist. Remember to try not to judge yourself! Again we can try to identify the patterns by listing them in your journal with the date.

Choosing a Response

With practice we can learn to respond instead of react. Just through continuing your Mindfulness practices you may have become more aware that you are not your thought or your emotion. You are much more than that and little by little you can distance yourself from them in order to make a choice that works best for you. So instead of being frustrated by someone who is late and ruminating that feeling of frustration until they arrive by creating a negative story around it because I'm feeling rejected, i can change my perspective of the situation and perhaps just decide to remain calm but ask them why they are late when they arrive.

Non-Violent Communication (NVC) as an approach to improving our communication with others, is a simple framework to understand theoretically but takes some practice. Its all about deciding to try something different. Like anything that takes us outside our comfort zone it can feel a bit strange initially. If you are truly looking for a more peaceful life with better relations then its worth persisting, it gets easier!

Recognize the times that you are most likely to have some of the reactions towards others mentioned earlier. Perhaps when you are tired or stressed? When you feel someone is not listening to you? Or you don't feel respected?

1. Notice the facts (what actually happened, not your interpretation of it! What was said?)
2. How do I feel about it (using your awareness skills, what do i feel in my body
3. What need might the situation be demonstrating to me (what would truly make me feel better? To be listened to? Or loved? Or do I need rest?)
4. What request can I make to the other person or to myself so I can feel better? (e.g. asking if both of you can take turns to speak and listen to the other person? Ask for a hug? Or perhaps simply get an early night)

When we give ourselves this space we can also do the same for others, and therefore understand that they also have needs. When two people make requests to each other from this more empathetic perspective then magical things can happen! We really all deep down have the same set of needs (but at differing times) so it's easier to meet at this level rather than getting caught up with who is right or wrong. Privileging the relationship tends to be more beneficial in the long-term, although having said that you can never force anyone else to change their behavior towards you. They are also free to choose a response. When we are more benevolent, the other person's actions towards us also tend to be more positive but if they are not then we can choose to be loving to ourselves and walk away.

Exercise in looking more objectively at a tense situation:

Think of a recent disagreement. Write down the following :

- The facts
- How do you feel?
- What need may lie behind that feeling?
- How could it have worked out better for you?

Complete the sentence.... *When i think of this situation, I feel.....*
because I need.....

Quick quiz : How might I satisfy these needs? These are just a few
examples.

- I feel tired (I choose to give myself rest)
- I feel angry (I choose to give myself calm, peace)
- I feel worried (I choose to provide myself with reassurance)
- I feel sad (I choose to provide myself with comfort, or to
  listen to what I feel is missing in my life)

How could I change that into a request I make to someone else?

- "I'm feeling too tired to give you my full attention right now,
  is it ok for you to talk in 15 minutes?"
- "I'm annoyed that you said *You are lazy*", i need some space
  to calm down"
- "I'm feeling anxious about my exam tomorrow. Would it
  be ok if i call you just before it starts as I will feel better if I
  have someone to talk to?"
- "I feel sad that we are saying goodbye, can we arrange to
  meet again soon?"

Practices such as NVC help us to develop empathy for other people.
We can, however, also do this in other experiential ways which
move us out of our prejudices. Every time we can recognize positive
qualities in others we take a step further to allowing ourselves also
to be more authentic in our connections with them.

Exercise in seeing the similarities with strangers:

When you are next sitting quietly in a coffee shop or a park, take a
moment to look more closely than you would normally at someone

else. Notice the similarities with yourself, even the basic things. Do they have two eyes? two arms? Same color eyes? See how many you can find.

Exercise in seeing the positive in others:

Think of someone who you have difficulty getting along with. Putting aside the difference for a moment, write down three things that you admire or appreciate about them. If you are having difficulty, then look at the characteristic that you believe to be negative and investigate around what positive aspects this person may also have in that case. For example, someone who you find difficult because you feel they are too demanding of you, may also be someone who is capable of rigour and attention to detail in their own tasks.

Projecting on Others : How does our mirroring work?

I've always liked listening to people's stories. Not the kind of day-to-day complaints, but the real deal. The way they've overcome difficulties to grow and see the gratitude in different situations, the contrast we talked about. They can be big or small. I find that other people's stories come up just at the right time, often as I'm working through something similar. We innately reflect each other so we're never alone in our journeys when we look around and connect with other people.

It can also be interesting to build our awareness of how we mirror and project on each other though. To get to a place of sovereignty or self-leadership, we need to own all of our responsibilities in the stories of our lives. It's about being both authentic in our interactions and avoiding placing our problems or the qualities we can't see in ourselves on others. So until we reintegrate the different parts of ourselves, like Osiris, we are either over-admiring or criticising these in other people.

We are all spiritual beings living a human life which means we experience the full range of emotions and characteristics. These emotions guide us, alerting us to our needs and desires. If we suppress them, or in other words refuse to feel a particular emotion, then we externalize the power associated with that emotion to listen to what it's telling us and therefore to act. We start to see that characteristic in other people and it triggers us. Take anger for example. A lot of people don't wish to be seen as an angry person, so much so that they refuse to even feel it, they label it as 'bad' or 'socially unacceptable'. Anger is just telling us about our boundaries though and is so strong because it's protecting us from being invaded or dominated in some way. It's part of our vital energy. It's really what we do with our anger that matters though, it doesn't have to overwhelm us.

So when we think of the other people in our lives and our relationships with them, it can be useful to look at what we might be projecting. Another way of saying this is what are you holding for me? If I refuse the presence of anger in me then I pass this on to someone else and quite often blame them at the same time : "you are angry" and I do this so I can really experience myself as being a "peaceful" person. I do this because I do not recognize my ability to operate within both of these realms of polarities. I label one as good and one as bad, and in doing so I choose a reference outside of myself to project that image onto. In terms of owning our own vital energy and our authenticity, this is not ideal. So we learn to take responsibility for our own projection on others. They will keep being angry towards you until each person owns their own projection. If you're finding yourself locked in recurring situations then this might be why. We are showing each other constantly what parts of us we need to accept. We bury emotions, talents, characteristics and ways of thinking in order to be acceptable in other's eyes. Taking back one's projections says, yes, I can also be or feel that way too and I still love and accept myself fully.

Exercise to see the difference and reintegrate it :

If I find myself blaming, attacking or disliking someone because of a characteristic then it is helpful to take a journal and write down why. Note down the particular characteristic which troubles you about them. What is the opposite of that characteristic? Ask yourself if this opposite is how you are experiencing yourself within the situation. So to illustrate, if you find the person to be aggressive, do you find yourself to be the peacekeeper? If you find them to be selfish, do you find yourself to be giving?

When in your life were you not allowed to express that so called negative behaviour? Can you recall a time when you did demonstrate the characteristic that troubles you (even if not in exactly the same way?). Were you told or did you feel that it was unacceptable? Offer that part of yourself compassion for having been isolated and rejected. As an adult you can welcome that part of you back like a nourishing parent because you no longer need to reject it.

Parents can project onto their children in this way because children are excellent mirrors. They show us everything that we denied ourselves, or felt that we were denied as children. The characteristics that we have given up in the name of socialization. Thus their follies annoy us because they are irresponsible, or daydreaming, or attention-seeking, to name but a few. What is the need behind their behavior: love? freedom? to be heard? Perhaps if we let ourselves daydream a little more we may feel more at peace with ourselves and them? We wouldn't judge it as inacceptable.

Following on from the idea of projection, we can see how we might fall into patterns with people which feel as if they are inevitable sometimes. They're not. As we continue our self-knowledge work we can become aware in particular of what we don't want to own. We make shifts both within those relationships and on an energetic level as we clear them. You have probably heard the expression of "taking a weight of your shoulders" when a conflict is resolved.

As one person works on themselves, the other may chose to grow or not. If the person we are mirroring chooses not to move out of the old dynamic then they may find someone else to project onto. This is why sometimes even if we change our circumstances by, for example, finding a new job, our relationship issues follow us around until we solve them.

If both shift into a higher understanding then the relationship can progress to learning something else, and since both people own their respective thoughts and projections then we arrive at the type of adult-adult relationships that a more evolved society needs.

We can also look at a case where someone might be projecting their more angelic qualities on someone else. Putting someone else on a pedestal is a good example. If we constantly look outside ourselves believing that what others are or have is better than our situation then we are essentially not seeing our own beauty, wonderful qualities or capacity to act to satisfy our needs. It's disempowering and not beneficial for our self-esteem when we neglect to see these qualities. We give our strength or our light away for example, leaving ourselves feeling weakened or inadequate over time. Neither are true, we simply need to give ourselves the opportunity to discover these qualities in ourselves.

Conscious analysis of our day-to-day interactions can help us to identify where we need to work. And remember, it is never a loving action to wish to control or use another person to satisfy our own needs. Every exchange between people should be based on the principle of free will.

When we can respond to projections in a way that is based on choice then we're becoming sovereign, emotionally balanced and able to maintain more adult-adult relationships. At this stage we can look at the situations in front of us with deeper understanding of the dynamics and more empathy. We unknit our co-dependencies on others to become more detached and able to fulfil our own needs. In the same way we suffer less from placing our expectations on them and this leaves space within the relationship to discover each other more authentically. Like Osiris, taking back those parts of ourselves makes us whole again, raising our awareness and allowing us to operate from a place of true self.

If you'd like to learn more about projections then *The Work* by Byron Katie is an excellent start, followed by an introduction on how to work with parts of our personality through an approach such as Internal Family Systems (IFS) developed by Dick Schwarz. This teaches us how to listen empathically to what our parts are trying to tell us in order to arrive at an informed choice, taken from a place of centredness. When we are taking decisions from this angle we are ready to truly meet others in wholeness and create harmonious interdependent environments.

Collective Intelligence

We live in a time where everyone is talking about collective intelligence. What is it and how can you participate fully? Why is it so important?

Collective intelligence is an approach which values the communal impact of data and knowledge that comes from a wide range of sources. Proponents claim that group intelligence is stronger than individual, translating through mutual recognition of what each person brings to the collective effort.

From a more spiritual standpoint, the shift to unity consciousness represents a mindset perspective, *"we are all one"* whereas collective intelligence translates this into the how/who. We're entering a phase where interdependence and co-creation will prime and these forms of working together will flourish.

Basically "no man is an island". We live in an age where the rate of progress and the associated amount of information available to us is exponential. The issues we face are complex in many cases and require sustainable solutions, developed to satisfy a wide audience. For this reason, it is vital to associate many different perspectives, sources of knowledge and experience. Recognising and indeed welcoming diversity is therefore a key principle for the future, not only for reasons of inclusion and acceptance which are important in themselves, but also to fundamentally create great solutions. Each contribution counts and we're essentially moving towards ensuring the respect of each individual within the collective. We are all unique within a connected network. It is important that each individual feels that it is possible to add their own shade of color. This is how we arrive at white light! It requires each individual to look within to find the gifts they wish to share and then an environment which facilitates their connection and interaction. Generally this will represent a minimal framework where indeed there are rules agreed upon by the group, but light enough to encourage creativity and contribution. Nature itself regulates according to basic laws of organization and the more we look to learn from her, the more we will progress in this area.

The importance of collective intelligence is almost a universally accepted principle today. Putting it into practice, however, can leave much to be desired. Teams with similar profiles tend to agree with each other since there is little challenging. Teams with differing values and experience often need longer to gel but it is generally accepted that they produce better results.

This is because we all have different 'maps' of our world which are based on what we've learnt both formally and through experience, our differing values and socio-cultural influences. As we change or 'upgrade' our belief systems these maps change. The more flexible and quick we are at doing that, the easier it is to interact with others, being open to alternative views. No more us versus them mindsets, it is simply a question of does this new data sit well with my truth?

When we know ourselves and develop skills, including empathy, to interact well with others, we operate in less fear-based patterns because we don't feel threatened by other's differing viewpoints. We connect through our hearts and humanity instead. Given that we are essentially social creatures, operating as part of a harmonious and trusting group also builds well-being. Everyone gains when we develop the ability to interact well. In a trusting group, individuals feel secure enough to admit mistakes, ask for help and share other vulnerabilities. This is how we learn. These teams know that feedback is always about the behaviour or what is being achieved together, never about the essence of the person. When we arrive at these levels of interaction, deviant behaviour is seen as sickness to be remedied by the person themselves with the help of other members. Today we see this behaviour as almost the norm. Tomorrow it will be the opposite.

Here is a small exercise for developing empathy :

- It would be ideal to be sitting in a café or a public area such as a park, somewhere calm but not alone. Think of a person with whom you have a close relationship. In your journal, write down 5 things that are similar about you and that person. Next think of another person that you know pretty well but you are not as close to. Repeat the exercise. Lastly, select someone in your vicinity. What similarities do you notice about them and either yourself, or the two other people that you selected in the first part of the exercise? Again try to write down 5 things. Preferably without staring obviously!

Developing empathy is about seeing the similarities rather than the differences. In this way we move out of fear and into connection and compassion.

Since we are all different, two things are important to keep in mind whilst collaborating with others :

1. We have different communication preferences (visual, auditory, kinaesthetic) so our communication should be adapted to all eventualities, and in general we like to learn through not just one of these methods. It's a good practice to validate what you have heard.

2. To keep our dialogue authentic, there are approaches we can use such as non-violent communication (NVC). Even with the best of intentions, sometimes our conversations lack deep connection. We get caught up in the drama. This is where NVC can help bring us back to a reference and re-open dialogue. It is usually better to positively and mutually influence people over the long-term through privileging the relationship rather than convincing or imposing your views on people. Such victories tend to be short-lived!

Our Vulnerability and Changing Roles

Having decided that we'd like to work with less hierarchy and more inclusion through approaches such as collective intelligence, there is invariably some re-organization of our labels and identities that happens. This can be quite a sensitive phase since we have often built so many expectations and day-to-day interactions around these roles that we play. Holding a space for ourselves to be vulnerable during transition or in giving ourselves the freedom to try out new activities is about being compassionate with ourselves.

Working on ourselves inevitably makes us feel vulnerable as we try new behaviours or find the courage to recognize and share our stories. The more we do, the more our heart opens and the more we realize that everyone has their parts that they feel uncomfortable about sharing with the world. We're not alone in that. Your story could profoundly touch someone else and help them to work through their own issues as we've seen.

In terms of new leadership, one of the areas where this can be particularly difficult is in the roles that we play because we have become so accustomed to defining ourselves according to social status and other people's expectations. For many of us having spent time climbing the organizational hierarchy, it can be a painful experience to shift into a new role with a flat hierarchy. It doesn't have to do necessarily with thinking we are any better than anyone else, although this could be part of it. It is more that we have attached such importance to the position and someones defined our whole identity, life and path around the role that it has become inseparable from how we see ourselves. You are not your role, you never will be, you are something much greater than that but we need to shed that identity in order to realize that we don't really need it and that we have so much more freedom without it. It's like a comfortable cage. We shouldn't under-estimate this phase in any transition, it's very delicate and having been through it myself, I can attest to its painfulness. It pushes all of our buttons about self-worth and fears of the unknown.

One of the models I like to look at to understand it is the SCARF model developed by David Rock which adds insight to the five areas of the human social experience. We're affected by them in differing ways : Status, Certainty, Autonomy, Relatedness and Fairness.

- Status refers to how we perceive our relative importance compared to others
- Certainty refers to our propensity to try to predict what will happen in the future
- Autonomy is our need to be able to act independently and so apply control
- Relatedness impacts our sense of belonging to a group or safety in the company of others
- Fairness expresses a concern for there to be a fair exchange between people

These aspects operate interdependently during times of change. Somehow understanding that these different aspects were at play allowed me to take a step back from the stories I was creating. We can go through all kinds of feelings of betrayal, rejection, jealously, anger, sadness and guilt with organizational changes that are imposed on us, but it can also be the case when we choose the change. There is a certain period of accepting the changes and discovering how they will impact you which can take time. This is where support systems are important and we can take stock of whether the environment we are in and the people around us are beneficial to our growth or not. If they are not then we need to be taking decisions to ensure our well-being is maintained.

We are particularly vulnerable at these moments so self-compassion is vital. Give yourself space to digest the change, listen to and trust any feelings that come up without judging them, use a mindful technique to stay in the present so that our mind is not creating all kinds of stories (because it most certainly will!), and little by little look for the new possibilities that the change could bring to your life. Try to list the potential positives and focus on how they are emerging.

For me there have been several moments where I have let go of my attachments to particular identities or roles that I've created for myself. It felt like dropping every notion of who I thought I was to be in a space of emptiness, not knowing what was next. It just felt like a necessary step to release the existing vision because it no longer felt right, I would have been lying to myself. That void is quite destabilising because it's as if everything is falling away and you're just stationary, sitting there in the moment. Knowing intimately that everything just changed. My body and soul are still there, it's my mind that has simply lost its current story and feels panic because of the need to create a new one. It's also a very creative space, however, because we see that we are free to be whomever we wish. I always cry deeply at these moments, firstly out of fear but also out of the loss. It is like a small death, and it takes me a lot of courage to let go, but ultimately I've learned that holding on to notions that don't help us anymore is far more detrimental. I take a deep breath, I sit with it to be wholly accepting of my vulnerability, to reconnect to the ever present stillness within and try to trust that there is something else to discover beyond the next step.

Emotionally, whatever the underlying social experience, we go through a cycle of reactions to any change. One such model of these phases is described by the Change Curve designed by Elisabeth Kübler-Ross.

The phases of change are experienced by people in differing durations and intensities. At the beginning of the curve we find ourselves in a state of descent which is generally counter-productive with a refusal to accept the new situation and an attachment to the past. Following this, we move into a state of ascension which is characterized by a more positive, forward-looking and productive stance.

The first stage is *shock* and often accompanied by a feeling of being stuck. In the second phase, we feel *denial*. Depending on the context, if this touches a delicate subject for the person then the denial will be stronger. It is protecting the person from having to start the phase of putting the old to rest. When moving into the next phase, the person feels *anger* at the injustice of the new situation, searching for a scapegoat to blame and in doing so taking on a victim posture. It is important to remember that this is perfectly normal but we need to move ourselves out of this phase in order to progress and this phase can be very typical of what we see within the collective and organizations as whole. Our anger can propel us forwards but in doing so we then face fear. Our *fears* of an uncertain context, people, of not feeling we'll be good enough for example. All of these can lead to anxiety and irrational behaviour.

Sadness, which is the next phase, shows us what was important to us in the old context. It can lead us into discouragement with "what's the point?" or even deep nostalgia and depression. Being aware of these possibilities can encourage us to try to look after ourselves and seek support, knowing that a "click" will happen at some point where we decide that we no longer wish to remain in this state and it shifts us into a phase of *acceptance*. In this moment, we decide to make do with or make the best of the situation. During this phase we also forgive ourselves and our guilt, along with potentially the other party whom we blamed by giving more understanding to why this might have occurred.

As this upward phase continues, we can see more and more positives in the new situation. We often say that at this stage we can *"get to the thank you"* so that we can see how we have grown and that it would not have occurred without the event. During the final phase, the change has been fully integrated and we find our enthusiasm for the new situation and all that it can bring us.

I found it useful to understand the process I was going through when facing various transitions in the past few years, both personal and professional. The most empowering part was in understanding when my energy was particularly low during the bottom of the curve and how we can slowly move this up through exercise or by working through the emotions rather than getting stuck in the story. It's also a time where I felt very much like hibernating, of pulling away from other people, when in fact the paradox was that in reaching out, I realized that there is always support available, and how many other people had similar stories or ones that were just as difficult and that was powerfully healing. Sharing our vulnerability can open our hearts further and connect us more deeply to others. To discover this, we need to drop the story we are telling ourselves about others : they won't understand, our story is different, we don't know how to tell it, they will judge us... We don't know until we move into courage in order to share it. We only have our pride to lose, and everything to gain in terms of shifting back up that curve to "seeing the thank you" and the feeling of peace associated with that. In many cases, others are also going through similar transitions and so will be encouraged also to share. The more we do this, the more it makes vulnerability a normal and acceptable characteristic for anyone to demonstrate.

Building Trust

Authenticity means being oneself in all circumstances. Realising that we are perfect as we are but can choose to keep growing or not. As we said earlier, it's about standing in one's truth : defining it, stating it, owning it and acting on it.

The importance of seeing and sharing one's truth is fundamental in developing a feeling of wholeness. It's underpinned by this authenticity because when we are operating in a coherent way we see the impact of who we truly are and adjust until we feel ourselves to be in harmony. A well-known way to approach this is to :

- Tell the truth to yourself about yourself
- Tell the truth to yourself about another
- Tell the truth to another about yourself
- Tell the truth to another about another, and
- Tell the truth to everyone about everything

Particularly when we are in transition, still developing our competencies for interaction, this doesn't have to be directly addressed to the person concerned. We can journal to see what our thoughts are or write a letter to the person but not send it! We often tell ourselves stories about life events or even just some of the day-to-day ups and downs which keep us in a state of drama. This drama creates separation with others and is a reflection of our need for more inner calm. The more we practice the form we give to our feedback, the easier it becomes to say what we need to in a benevolent but authentic way. Learning how to give authentic and positive feedback that builds rather than weighs on relationships is absolutely key.

When giving feedback to others :

- It's always about the behaviour and not the person, use benevolence
- We remain as factual as possible, avoiding judgement and subjective criticism
- Include the hypotheses on which we are basing our feedback so the person can understand our reasoning
- Try to provide feedback as soon as possible after the event
- Only use "I" statements to own your observations and feelings. It will seem less like an attack on the person. Doing this also avoids generalisations such as "you always…"
- The feedback is on the effect that the person's behaviour has on you which is why it is pertinent

When receiving feedback from others :

- Initially just listen and don't interrupt
- Ask for context (when, what, how…)
- Listen actively and recap what you have heard
- Try to avoid replying with *"yes but"* as this is a half-hearted excuse, you are not trying to win the person over, only accept or reject their feedback depending on if it is pertinent to you. If you feel judged then it is healthy to express that instead of keeping it for yourself, but state why and then look into why you may be reacting defensively.
- If the person is providing feedback based on an area in which he or she has expertise then ask for support from them to adjust the behaviour, expressing any difficulties that you feel so that they are aware and can provide pertinent guidance
- Always say thank you! Feedback is a gift that someone gives to you, even if it can sometimes feel harsh.

Trusting Ourselves

I find it difficult to imagine how we can trust other people if we don't trust ourselves. As a caring person I had imagined that I automatically trusted other people. Intellectually I did. I delegated, I trusted that their actions and words would be well-intentioned. This was my deep love of humanity talking but I realized during my journey, that despite that benevolent stance, part of me was frightened of their reactions, of their judgement. The shyness that I had created as a protection for myself as a child was telling me that fundamentally I was creating a barrier between myself and others, an excuse for not fully engaging. That meant that I was probably not quite as open and trusting as I thought I was and that was quite an eye-opener for me. So I worked on opening up by calming my inner critic with Mindfulness practice and by looking at the judgement that I had about myself, about needing to be perfect, to always do and say the *right* things. So I tapped on those with EFT or

I looked at my polarity of judgement to find those moments where I had severally judged myself and asked myself if it was really an accurate picture, changing my frame of reference into something far less impactful. In doing this kind of work and getting to the thank you the situation for having brought us something new, our heart spaces start to open more and more, releasing old fears. People can inherently feel this openness. When we are comfortable with ourselves, that is what we also resonate to others without having to say a word. This is why authenticity is important to a heart-centred leader because it just emanates. Being before doing.

There is also the question of trusting our intuition. As we let go of needing to control situations and move into surrender we also become more trusting in ourselves and that inherently things will fall into order without us needing to force. In acceptance we can just be in the present, wholly available to what and who we are working with and listening to our inner guidance without being polluted by our stories.

Exercise for learning to trust our inner guidance :

- During one of your journaling sessions, try to recollect a moment where you had an intuition about something and you didn't follow up on it? What happened? How did you feel? Why did you doubt it? List some reasons why you might be afraid to follow up on your intuitions?
- Now decide upon a period of time during which you will commit to following your intuitions. It doesn't need to be very long. To do so take a brief moment of calm to connect into your inner truth but try to avoid thinking into the question. Note down what happens each time. What happened? How reliable was your inner compass?

Flowing through life is about surrender, listening to one's inner compass. Accepting what is and then choosing a course of action as a consequence, especially when we acknowledge what life brings to us naturally as a consequence of letting go of trying to control everything. We can try to control every eventuality but if we do we will spend most of our precious time fixing issues and feeling stressed. We end up tired and not necessarily taking the best course of action for our well-being, we lack perspective and use our energy in drama rather than in positive actions that are constructive and bring us joy. When we are not trying to control others or our circumstances, and we place our energy on nobler intentions such as aligning thought, word and action people feel the authenticity.

Establishing authentic dialogue also develops trust with others. But trust extends over and above what we say. Trust means different things to each of us. Again we sometimes naturally expect that others will operate in the same way as we do and yet they often see the world differently. Building up trust with others therefore requires us to be flexible.

We can look at trust through the four lenses of the DISC personality types. Personally, I don't like boxing, but here it will help just to illustrate how our perspectives may differ. Which of the following traits may apply to the way you believe that we demonstrate trust? :

- D : Showing capability and credibility through knowledge and impactful action; Inspiring confidence through achieving results, leading and by transferring feedback and knowledge to others
- I : Acting with integrity and truthfulness in decision-making and actions; keeping confidences; being fair and objective in the treatment of others
- S : Ensuring that others feel they belong, are valued and encouraged to participate; listening to and sharing

information; caring for the well-being of others; building relationships

- C : Valuing consistency and reliability; demonstrating timeliness, attention to detail and commitment; respect of procedures and rules

As we go about our day-to-day, we are continually evaluating whether another person's behaviour adheres to our mental maps or not. Were they late for an appointment with us? Did they do what they said they would? Did they divulge a secret? Did we feel included in a discussion? When we understand what other people may value, we can learn to not take their behaviour so personally when it doesn't match our vision of what is right or wrong. It is simply a different perspective as we saw earlier. As we get to know each other and work with different people, if we keep an open mind we deepen our understanding of others and their needs. Observing non-judgementally and listening is key. In doing so we can better respect this diversity and therefore benefit both personally and through our collective efforts.

Active Listening and Deepening Dialogue

Gerald Jampolsky once described deep listening with undivided attention and unconditional love as the greatest gift that we can give to another person. We're generally so busy with our schedules and our gadgets that we don't take the time to sit fully present to another person and what they have to share with us. To treat their words as important because the person is important.

Active listening takes practice. If you have learnt a new language and spent time immersed in a new country listening to native speakers all day long then you will see the similarities. When I moved to France, I remember many an occasion in the first month of falling asleep at the dinner table in the evening after concentrating so hard to understand everyone. Well, training yourself to listen to each person can be like this at first. Simply put aside any distractions and resolve to listen and give your whole focus to the person. You can refer to the earlier exercise of not jumping in to speak if you find it helps. Just let yourself be there with them, without any need to prove yourself or reply in any way. We need to strongly pull our attention back each time our mind wanders, but in the same way as most things in life, it gets easier with practice until it becomes second nature.

Applying these techniques to interviews and group work can have particularly impactful results. People who are deeply listened to feel in a trustful and safe space and will share so much more if there are also rules around confidentiality. In more innovative corporate environments we can use these techniques to help teams to share their difficulties and establish more authentic conversations before moving onto co-creating their story. For this reason, they can be particularly useful in the face of continually resurfacing problems where frustrations are not being expressed. Best accompanied by a facilitator such as through the Institute of Cultural Affairs, the group develop a collective field of sharing which takes them beyond the idea of good or bad, or us versus them, to explore common key subjects without fear of judgement. As a space simply to share, these sessions shouldn't target results, decisions or actions. They are moments outside of the usual day-to-day to allow people to express and practice actively listening to the underlying feelings and values of the work and environments they are co-creating.

The way forward: Navigating Uncertainty Through Community

We talked about diversity and contrast and their importance to understanding ourselves and others. Here we further address the question of interdependency to look at how both my and your happiness can be achieved without the need to dominate. We need to start by asking ourselves the question of what if life wasn't a zero-sum game? Meaning what if my gain didn't mean that you necessarily have to lose? That win-win situations do exist very often if we stay in a creative and open state of mind. Why is there still so often the idea that everything is insufficient in the world so we need to compete to get ahead? Fortunately mindsets are changing and we are thinking more about quality than quantity. What is most important to me is not necessarily as important to you so there's always room to listen and discuss more deeply in any situation. This means being strong enough to step away from fear-driven actions. Again, developing awareness of our dynamics helps here.

Wouldn't it be great to belong to a global family who move and shake! Who use their gifts and competencies to express who they are and not to be better than another. Using our choices in an assertive way that speaks really of who we are, what we agree or don't agree with, and what we are part of changing. Being part of a community means belonging to a positive and progressive movement. Such communities could easily represent a force for placing joy, creativity and the celebration of life at their core. These are all things we appreciate. Lets put these at the centre of all that we share with the world every day!

To do this we need to remove much of the judgement that plagues our self-esteem and attitudes that put others down. When we're comfortable with ourselves, we don't feel a need to do that. And in any case, it's such a waste of precious energy that could be used for making our lives better. In guiding our lives in the right direction, our time, energy and thoughts are extremely precious so cultivate a like-minded, positive circle of friends or colleagues.

Again, don't judge. we've all been through rough patches that make it harder to smell the roses. What we're suggesting is to be aware of the company we keep generally so we're not pulled into negative ways of talking or frames of mind. A lot of the time people don't even realize they are doing it. It's just a habit. Mindfulness or other awareness training helps us to be conscious, not just of our own thoughts but also of the environment within which we reside. Put your choices and energy into places where you feel you can belong, where your contributions are appreciated. Really, we have better things to do than to stay in environments which are counterproductive to supporting our sovereignty... Take your time to find the right tribe for you!

Paul Born in his book "Deepening Community: Finding Joy Together in Chaotic Times" distinguishes between shallow, fear-based and deep communities. Shallow communities have no emotional connection and interaction is almost transactional. Fear-based communities attract members because of their us versus them attitude of discrimination against non-members. A deep community meanwhile exhibits a shared identity, with interest in others through shared stories, caring for one another, and acting together for the benefit of all. If we are to progress on the journey to authenticity and wholeness then we need to be able to be the same person in all circumstances, including within our teams and organizations. This is where the conditions of deep community can provide environments in which people can flourish.

Many traditional communities use the power of dialogue and mutual support as their basis. I came to discussing some typical practices with a guide when visiting a Malaysian national park. He talked about the importance of their morning meetings for expressing and collectively solving problems to avoid arguments or resentment. That helping each other out was given an important place, not just in these sittings but in the general day-to-day.

We live in an ever more complex world where information and technology are evolving at an exponential rate. How do we keep up? The answer lies certainly in not franticly chasing and absorbing a maximum of knowledge as there will always be too much. Life is asking us to go back to first principles and know (1) that we already know what we need to in a lot of cases in order to follow our paths. Much of what we take in daily is fear-based and superfluous. It is our fear of not being aware of everything and a wish to control our circumstances that encourages us to stay hyper-connected (2) when we do need to co-create then it's a key competency to know where to find information and how to connect with people who know complementary things. Uncertainty in our lives causes us a certain amount of fear until we learn to go with the flow, to listen to what life is telling us. But it is also encouraging us to connect with others, and I believe that great constructive teams and communities get the best results. So how do we as individuals learn to function well as part of a co-creation? In the previous chapters we have talked about the importance of authenticity, so rule number one is to be yourself. Combined with the form of sharing that we found in the earlier sections on collaborating, this should give us a solid basis for entering any circle.

As we set out in co-creating it is important that the group agree on the intention. Why are they there and what unites them? They will then decide on where to go. Know fundamentally why you want to contribute to a particular project. In these shifting times, the how we get there doesn't matter as much. Even if we set a plan it will definitely change so we're looking more to develop a sense of direction (or purpose) for ourselves and the project, whilst keeping flexibility in our day-to-day. We can compare this to *tacking* (or *beating*) that is used in sailing where we zig-zag around a particular direction because we cannot progress headlong into the on-coming wind. As long as it's the right direction and we don't keep changing our minds then we can use the changing winds to head in the right direction.

As we choose the people to work with, we need to look at two aspects. Firstly to ensure that we have similar values and secondly to distinguish between the notions of *competencies* and *preferences* as these are what they will bring to the project. We discussed values earlier so let's look now at preferences and competencies.

A *preference* is a natural inclination you have towards certain activities. With these you can find yourself in a state of flow and so they give you energy. As we saw in the values section, the more we are doing the things we love, the more our wellbeing increases. It's a virtuous circle. *Competencies*, by contrast, are developed. I may have a preference for drawing or math but I still need to spend time working to develop that skill.

In making this distinction, team members can allocate different tasks in a project to each other according to whether they suit their preferences (e.g. I may enjoy detailed work, whilst you may enjoy creativity). We can feel reticent to ask others to take on tasks that we don't enjoy, they may just prefer them so don't hesitate to discuss! Reallocating tasks optimally like this can increase a team's energy level phenomenally. It is important to keep in mind a person's need to develop their competency in a particular area of preference also, by providing opportunities and giving them space. If it aligns with their preference then they should develop quickly.

If we are each honest with ourselves then we will find the project which motivates us and therefore we can contribute best to and also grow from our participation.

For particularly big projects, it can be important to establish a combined sense of purpose. Perhaps look at how our individual stories brought us to this particular project in order to also understand our place and maintain a good level of intrinsic motivation. Establishing this sense of purpose allows us to be clear and impactful in our actions. Acknowledging our individual stories together then allows us to co-create a new story built around joint intention.

Of course these stories evolve at different rates so it can create tension. Every co-creation is like a recipe. The ingredients each need to be lovingly prepared before they can be combined so the masterpiece can unfold. The eggs may need to be whisked so they can transform into an omelette (and I mean whisked, not beaten, broken or cracked!). They may need time to adjust to their new way of being before being combined with the other ingredients, each themselves having gone through their unique transformation. They come together either in a specific order or through improvisation. Some may need to wait. Yes, we need to give others space to do their thing sometimes before we get to add our special touch! That's the beauty of it if we can stand back and look at the bigger picture without getting involved in drama and competition. It's neither competition, nor a race to produce quality innovations and solutions together. What emerges in the end is what counts, and it's bigger than just me.

But what happens if the eggs don't show up? The ham and the cheese have a choice, always to look around for other eggs because they really feel they'd like to to be part of an omelette or to decide to transform into a sandwich instead where perhaps they were meant to be the star of the show this time. Some of the best culinary inventions of our time have come through missing ingredients, breaking the 'rules' to try something new so be careful of misconceptions of the way things 'have to be' and trying to over-control the process. It brings rigidity, stress and stagnation. In our complex and changing world we need fluidity around the basic structure. Emerging the highest potential requires that space. It requires discovery, feeling what we want to collectively emerge, deeply listening to what each ingredient can contribute and understanding how they can do that in their current form. Once the eggs are boiled, there is no point in trying to force them to become an omelette. How often do traditional organisations try this or not even notice the transformation within the shell. We rarely got below the surface of seeing each other. In facilitation we often say to trust that the right people are in the room. What needs to emerge will do so. You can always tell how much love has been put into a recipe and how well the ingredients are respected and ultimately combine.

So when are we ready to prepare the recipe? How do we know how long to wait? Either the group comes together and tries, or benevolently decides based on their hopes and needs whether they are ready. There needs to be a helicopter perspective and a sense of realism in where we might be able to go together. This is where our ability to see our current reality without drama is key. Heart-centred leaders have the capability of seeing the highest potential of each ingredient. They operate from a place of benevolent realism and creativity at any one time. They can see the possibilities, share options with the group on what they see emerging, listen, combine. They have patience and they care passionately about the final co-creation. This could be said of any member of the team when there is authentic dialogue in place. When operating from a higher place, we're willing to put in the love it takes to get us where we need to go in order to allow the best creation to unfold. This is a difficult concept to implement whilst we are still in a mode of trying to fix and control our results with stories of how, why, what, where and when. We need to trust people and processes more, if people's values align with the project then they will show up. But do bear in mind to keep our compassion and sense of humour to hand as everyone has the occasional bad day!

There are two aspects to great teams. One is the composition as we've seen earlier based on competency and diversity of viewpoints, the other is how they take decisions and therefore the speed at which they progress.

In these uncertain times, the key is either to delegate a decision because someone has the competence to deal with it and therefore we trust their judgement. This would be the typical case of a flatter hierarchy. Alternatively, there may be strong interdependencies in the impact of the decision. Although I understand how the newer committees where these impacts are debated may be of use in progressing, I'm not convinced that they always help us to take the right decisions.

I see many postings talk about the importance of being factual, and indeed facing facts and the apparent reality of a situation is key. Personally, however, I will always leave space for discussing people's strong intuitions. Many people whom I have met, especially entrepreneurs are strongly guided by these inner compasses and to neglect them would be a big danger. We need to use all of our abilities and indeed being whole means we don't neglect any part of them. It is easy to see the difference between someone who is simply being opinionated and someone who has an intuition about which way to go. The former can argue for hours about why their approach is correct, the latter is more authentic in its presentation, and may not even be able to explain the why, it's just a state of knowing.

The important thing is that the *right* decision is taken for the group, not that it is taken quickly and that the team backs the response that is chosen. When we use the term *right* it also means for that moment in time, and not that other actions would be necessarily wrong. We simply make a *choice* together and then we stand by it because we trust each other and we know that there is flexibility to adapt to circumstances if progress appears to be deviating from the required outcome. This will happen when people are involved in the decision and have some implication in how the approach is implemented. We are less in circumstances that require a rapid *event-decision-action* looping which is individual and more in co-creation to bring more balanced and impactful outcomes. Back-tracking on rigid decisions can be expensive in these times of uncertainty so allow mistakes and build trust in order to allow teams to steer themselves through long projects.

Exercise in Co-Creation Methods : Liberating Structures

When we wish to co-create and at the same time respect each member's participation in a process, then we can solicit a high level of engagement though activities such as Liberating Structures (**www. liberatingstructures.com**).

These facilitation techniques are simple to learn and can be applied to many contexts in a practical manner. The idea is that they are detailed and simple enough for anyone to use provided that people are open-minded about trying out alternatives to traditional presentations and mundane meetings because they are interactive.

There are 33 different possibilities which can be combined in order to achieve particular results with a group. They are fun with a purpose!

CREATE

Sparking Personal Creativity

Creativity forms the very essence of who we are as human beings. Everything that we think, speak and do is filled with the potential and the energy to become something new and therefore is an act of creation. At any moment in time we are inventing, whether it's a sentence, a new idea, solving a problem, or we're physically creating an object. You are giving form to energy in a way that is unique, and therefore this expresses something unique about you.

Authors and artists throughout history have talked about gaining inspiration for their creations from the world and people around us. These are subconsciously mixed with all of our prior experience and essence to bring forward a new insight or idea. We need to be willing to take small risks to let the new emerge and in doing so discover something about ourselves. Allowing ourselves to step out of our comfort zones to discover is where the magic starts. Believing is seeing!

From the point of view of self-leadership, rediscovering our creativity not only helps to develop both the left and right hemispheres of the brain, but fundamentally it is empowering to know that we can develop our capacity to change anything that doesn't suit us. When we see ourselves as creative so many more possibilities and solutions suddenly open up to us. Imagination is limitless.

Since we have established that we're all creative, how about we look at how we can develop more creativity and incorporate new elements into our lives, our families, our organizations? The starting point is to have fun with it! The great thing about creativity is that it doesn't have to have a specific purpose when we set out. It's just an adventure to enjoy. A way of trying new things and seeing what comes out of that and how it makes us feel. So especially if you never saw yourself as creative, these exercises will help you to take some inventive first steps. For those of you who already see yourself as creative, well, the possibilities are of course endless! The question is whether we are making the time to nourish our creativity?

Create and recreate little or big, as you wish. It's just about giving yourself the utter freedom to try new things. This can be hard at first, as with any time we change habits or step out of our comfort zone because we can be creatures of habit. So here is a very practical approach which can help to move us into action and can be applied to just about any idea, activity or object that you'd like to evolve :

SCAMPER

Many innovations were born from simply making a slight change to the overall original composition of an object or idea. The SCAMPER approach offers us a structured way of seeing how creative we can be just by applying one of six possibilities. In this way we can experience something in a new way, even if it's just our outfit or the way we travel to work.

S for Substitute : Replace one of the usual elements by something else. Change the color, the shape, the texture, the smell, the pattern, change an ingredient. Alternatively you can simply try applying something in a different place or change your attitude towards it (for example, try preparing your salad differently by replacing an ingredient).

C for Combine : Combine two or more different ideas or elements to create a fresh new idea. Can I mix one theme or discipline with another to emerge something new? Combining ideas cross-discipline is creating so many new possibilities in terms of discoveries. What other elements can I bring in to provide a lift or some contrast? (for example, I enjoy meeting a friend for dinner but we often go to the same place. I also enjoy watching films and so does she, so alternatively I could propose that we stay at home and watch a film together to add some variety).

A for Adapt : adjust or rework an element. Transform it into something new perhaps by adding something that will emphasize it. Consider having the element adapted by a professional. Color it differently? Think about what the element looks similar to? Look at how others have transformed the same element, perhaps it will give you ideas. For example, how about creating a wall-hanging of various photographs that you have instead of them being hidden in an album or stored away electronically.

M for Magnify : ask yourself how you can exaggerate your idea for example by increasing the size, the print, the quantity, the intensity of, or the feeling it generates. Try a stronger perfume? Can I emphasize other areas of my idea by using contrast? Try layering ideas for effect. For example, in presentations, it can be useful instead of words to place a large impactful image in order to convey a key idea.

P for Put to Other Uses : What else could my idea or element be used for? Where could I use it that I don't today? How might someone else use it (look at blogs)? Might someone else make good use of this item if I can't? Here we might, for example, recycle an object or use household containers such as old bottles and bowls as alternative vases.

E for Eliminate : Remove an element from your routine or from an object. Does it become easier or more gentle, fluid? What does simplifying lines or ideas feel like? What are the essential parts of my creation? Are there non-essential elements that detract from or negatively impact the rest? If you are someone who often follows the same routine or process without challenging whether it is still optimal then try to see if you can eliminate any parts without losing its effectiveness. Perhaps it has been done that way for as long as you can remember! Iterate in order to evaluate the impact. Simplifying should bring clarity and help us to feel lighter.

R for Reverse (or Rearrange) : Consider swapping elements around. Just for fun, investigate how shapes or colors on the top or bottom half of your body influence your image. Perhaps reorder what you want to express by stating your request first and then qualifying it if you have a tendency to do the opposite, just to see whether you have the same reaction from people. Rearrange the order of the items on your desk or in a room of your home to see or experience them differently. You could even switch around your routine itself in order to add some freshness to your day!

To now go one step further, I'd invite you to look at the journaling tips we discussed at the very beginning if you haven't already managed to do so. Journaling is an excellent tool for developing self-awareness and self-expression through both writing and art.

World famous artist's coach Julia Cameron recommends writing three pages each morning to clear our heads of all those polluting thoughts and just see what emerges ("The Artist's Way", 2002). After a while, we find that there is less of a need to vent or outline our to-do list in those pages and this leaves space for soul searching. This is the process that I used to start writing articles on topics that I felt very deeply about and through it I also discovered my love of writing poetry. Regularity is key. Behind the drama and the mundane of the initial thoughts that need to be externalised, we find the same silence we encounter in meditation. Here again lies a doorway to our true self. This is the quiet space that we want to tap into in order to express who we are at our deepest level. Try journaling at least a few lines per day for the next 21 days as a target, giving yourself a little time each morning or last thing at night to write whatever comes without censoring. It helps to unblock our creative flow. It's very important not to judge what comes up, again be conscious but gentle on yourself. Nothing stops the flow of creativity more quickly and effectively than judgement!

Then when we touch our essence, we realize like all of life, it's changing, evolving as we experience and grow. By looking again and again we can dip into that place of self-knowing to experiment and express different facets of who we are.

Now that our creative juices are flowing, we can start to apply our creativity more widely to bring freshness and empowerment to our lives. The very act of putting oneself into action without judgement opens a whole world of possibilities.

It seems also that the more powerful the emotion involved, then the greater the impact of that which is created. Since we know that emotions are energy, it may well be that since we are such empathic creatures we can sense the feeling that the creator wished to convey. So how might we listen our own emotions, needs and dreams to create in a powerfully personal way? How might we channel them into co-creations that infuse our passions to contribute, learn new things and grow?

I believe that the act of choosing to re-create oneself in order to experience something else about our nature is the very essence of life. In doing so we need to let go of the past and our outdated view of who we are and associated objects and attachments in order to let the new emerge. As we have said earlier, this is not always an easy process, it takes surrender and humility to let the new come. The more we become willing to let things emerge through us individually, the easier it is to meet others in order to co-create.

In creating, we can move through ranges of feelings from guilt (*"I should be doing something more productive with my time"*, to fear (*"what if I can't remember how to create"*, to pride (*"what will people think of what I create"*), to eventually finding the courage to act and persist, trusting the fact that what emerges is a very personal part of who we are that merits to exist for that and no other reason, just as we do. In passing each phase or in trying to maintain a regular practice, we may bump into resistance. Noticing our resistance allows us to remind ourselves of why we set out on our journey in the first place and make the conscious choice to continue.

Life cycles and resistance

Life is change, moving with the times and what is right for you in every renewed moment. Being ok with that. But more than that, imagine we could learn to not just be ok but thrive as each season rolls around. Flowing with the cycles of life is as much about surrender as the ability to recreate oneself. Depending on the seasons, we may want to reflect the way we feel about our changing environments and the effect that it might have on our wish to hibernate or get out there and shine. The creative process itself has a very similar cycle to that of nature.

Let's first look at why sometimes we might not flow as swimmingly with change as a happy salmon in a river! Some form of resistance is generally the culprit. But no use going into guilt as it doesn't serve much so I'll share a story instead. I came across the feeling quite strongly this summer when I was at a yoga flow retreat. It was coming to the end of a fabulous week of practice and sharing, all based around the important theme of harmony. Yet there I was on the penultimate day, looking at my yoga mat staring unsympathetically back at me as I embraced yet another downward dog. I was feeling decidedly grouchy. That particular posture must have lasted at least 10 seconds longer than the teacher had promised, and my legs were feeling about as stable as a newborn camel. I was in the middle of an idyllic setting, with great teachers, I was progressing, yet in that moment did I feel my heart swelling with gratitude and positive karma? That's a very big no. Instead my arms were trembling like our world-famous British jelly and I was most definitely asking myself why at 6am I wasn't sitting quietly in some make-shift nest hugging my morning coffee instead. And then something just clicked. I realized I was in resistance and that if I stayed in that frame of mind and ruminating beliefs of "it's hard" or "why am I doing this?" that it wasn't going to get any easier and the class would seem endless. Yes I was tired but what I was actually doing was draining my energy and making the feat even harder. Have you been there?

So I had a choice. I'd already decided to come to the class (although, as a responsible adult I could of course just leave). I could also decide to enjoy it. So I concentrated on my breath, on the music, on flowing into the movement, on just being with my pose, in the present. In that instant both my bad mood and my thought that I wasn't enjoying the session subsided. I let go of clinging to my resistance and it dissolved. I couldn't identify with it anymore. Moments later I was in flow and not only enjoying the moment again but I could no longer feel the trembles or discomfort. Instead of my whole body mirroring my resistance it was naturally aligning to where my balance in plank pose was almost supporting me effortlessly. A humbling reminder of the power of breathing through our difficult moment to find a greater version of ourselves on the other side.

Whether on or off the mat, we make these choices at any and every moment. I'm not suggesting everyone gets into plank pose and starts breathing, but we can decide how to experience each moment. In resistance or in harmony with our environment. Yet bear in mind that what we resist persists.

What makes us resist?

1. Fight or flight : when the brain stem is engaged then we cannot be in a place of flow. It's a place of fear and survival, so we can have a tendency to want to turn and run, or become aggressive perhaps, or simply freeze up. Imagining alternatives isn't really an option at that moment so we first need to calm down. This is where breathing is particularly useful, along with mindfulness practices so we can be at least aware of the fact that we're emotionally highjacking ourselves!

2. Lacking direction or motivation : what do I want and why am I doing this are absolutely key questions. We talked about them in the volume on intention so feel free to try those exercises again, perhaps in a different context? Not being clear about the "what's in it for me?" question can lead to procrastination and ruminating doubts. It can also raise annoyance or frustration from not doing what we'd really like to. When we can remind ourselves of why we started in the first place then it can help renew our commitment during those difficult times, provided our goals were realistic and achievable. Having said that, when we push ourselves through resistance, we often realize we're capable of much more than we'd initially have imagined.

3. The inner critic : "It won't make any difference, what's the point, you'll never manage"

Heart-focused breathing exercise to put ourselves in coherence (and therefore move us out of fight-flight):

- Focus your attention on your heart area and think of a positive moment or experience or someone you care about in your life
- Breathe in slowly for 5 seconds and out for the count of 5 seconds, repeating for 3 minutes ideally

Aikido is also an excellent practice for learning about the strength and wisdom to be gained from non-resistance.

Here are some systemic questions now that we're calm to investigate how we can break through our barriers:

- Is the problem clear? What are the facts?
- Ask yourself how you would approach this problem in an ideal world?
- What is the benefit you gain from not doing anything? What will happen if nothing changes? Truly do you want to change the situation?
- Is there an option that you haven't yet tried? Is there an issue that you could have overlooked?
- What resources would you need to overcome the problem? Who needs to be involved?
- What first steps could you take? Are you doing anything that is counter-productive? How could you change that to turn the barrier into a positive learning experience?

Investigating Anger as a Driver For Change

We can't talk about recreating the new without taking an honest look at a particularly strong driver in the motivation to recreate an aspect of ourselves, anger.

One of the hardest things for me to do on this path of self-discovery was to accept my anger. It's one of our aspects that frequently tends to be suppressed to concentrate on developing the lighter aspects of our nature. Yet part of being human is accepting our vulnerabilities and also all of our parts and that includes the fact that we can be prone to anger, jealously, greed and other supposed 'sins'. We've always said that it's not healthy to bottle things up and my fundamental belief is that it makes us ill when we do. I'd been told on several occasions about needing to cleanse because I was holding toxins even if you'd never be able to tell from the outside. And frankly I've actually done lots and wasn't sure it was really having an effect. Toxins are a sign of holding on to negativity which festers and self-harms. Resentment is a big one here and it's just untreated latent anger. As we've said before it's always about you.

So what is resentment? It's essentially built up, underlying anger that has not been dealt with. It's all those times that I let my boundaries be crossed and in my case it was because I used to think that being easy-going and kind in all circumstances was the way to a happy life. Underlying this, however, was the erroneous belief that this is how I'd be loved, by being the model child and that meant being accommodating. What it served was frustration for what I felt as a lack of empathy for my needs. Since if I could do that, why didn't other people just do it automatically without me having to ask? This was before I realized that it was up to me to fulfil them. I judged their excessive reactions and need to impose their view as being limit violent and unnecessary. Such judgements represent a barrier to us being able to accept our own ability to demonstrate anger and when we do, we subsequently feel guilty about it.

The truth is that their anger scared me to some degree. Not in terms of what I experienced but in acknowledging what it meant to me. I can perfectly hold my own in an argument, but on a deeper level their demonstration was showing me a part of myself that I preferred to ignore and pretend wasn't there. I imagined that recognising my own anger meant a threat to destabilising what I felt was my wisdom and better judgement. How can we be fair and see all sides of an argument if we're losing our temper?

What I was actually doing was projecting this part of me on others and in doing so also denying a fundamental and very strong source of my vital energy. Anger is our motor to change what doesn't suit us, and is therefore an extremely strong compass to help us direct and verbalize what's not working. The important thing is what form or outlet to give it. So the question is not whether it's ok for it to exist in me, for me to feel it and listen to it, that goes without saying. But rather, what to do with it? As someone who had been taught to be kind and benevolent to others, this was a very perplexing challenge for me.

To make matters worse, I spent many, many years feeling like I'd been a rather turbulent teen. To anyone outside the house I was a model student and a supportive friend but when it came to what I experienced as any injustice at this age, I became extremely angry. As I grew through my teens I suppressed this part of me. I'd grown wiser and didn't need to act this way anymore, after all I was now a balanced adult who could reason and discuss rather than yell. What I did was to label this attitude and this part of my history as negative and hide it away. Instead, I could have looked at it as a moment where I was actually crying out for help to know how to manage my strong feelings, convincing myself I was unheard despite my parents efforts. I was incapable at the time of articulating that fundamental need for equality and justice that I was not feeling, lost as a middle child in a newly composed family of five kids, most of whom were the same age. The more I yelled, the more I alienated my brothers and sisters and subsequently this became a moment in my life when I separated psychologically to a small extent from the people who I love the most.

Life being what it is, this separation propelled me on my way to going out into the world to discover from an early age. It fuelled my search for different cultures, religions and ultimately philosophies of what was 'correct' or 'incorrect' behaviour or ways of being. I was looking for perfection and expecting it of myself instead of giving myself a break. It made me for a while judgemental of any people or behaviours that didn't seem benevolent to others.

What I understand now is that anger is most definitely a part of me like it is every single person on this planet, and it's a vital one. As we said earlier, it is how I choose to listen to it that matters. So, what can we do?

Even with Non-Violent Communication was allow ourselves to vent as an act of both self-compassion and human necessity, but we name it as such. I'm just venting. This needs to come out before we can calm down and get to the real underlying need. Two or three minutes of venting might be sufficient, after that we're probably projecting on the other person so there is something more fundamental to clear. Perhaps an invitation to dig into that to understand what story we're playing out.

This is not an open invitation to get angry with anyone and everyone, to be violent or abusive. That's not what I'm suggesting. Today I simply recognize that anger is an unmet need. The more violent it becomes, the more obvious it is that the person is in difficulty, sometimes repeating unconscious patterns that haven't yet been accepted and healed in themselves. As we know, abusers have often themselves been abused.

Today I can stand in front of anger and see that the person's words and actions represent their own journey and unmet need. I sometimes find it hard to listen deeply in the moment, but I keep the intention of trying to understand what the underlying issue is, separating the venting from what the person might really be asking of me. Is part of it reasonable and give us the potential to meet them in a new space which builds the relationship for both sides? Can I put aside my pride in order to find the courage to do that? Or is part of the reaction simply their history or a different way of seeing the world? We can also agree to disagree. In particular if there is abuse involved we can refuse to take that on. In doing so, that is accepting my own boundaries and needs whilst also being firmly loving with the other person. Love is not accepting all things. Having the strength to hold a mirror for someone else can also help them to see the issue they are not confronting, and the underlying unsatisfied need. Only when we authentically recognize and accept it as a part of us can we heal it and welcome it back as part of the wholeness of who we are. Peace is a choice we all make by working through that anger. There is no right or wrong, only stories we tell ourselves.

Working through latent anger :

1. Anger needs verbalisation in order to be recognized in the body. It is also a way of giving ourselves the freedom to just feel what we do without judgement. To authorize ourselves to step outside of the prisons we create for ourselves and that society imposes around what is acceptable or not. I suggest you place yourself away from the person until you have practiced verbalising in a way that owns your story, starting from "I"

2. Try keeping a diary of your moments of anger to understand what triggers them

3. Pretty much anyone who feels angry also feels guilty about it afterwards. It's essentially a way of self-punishment. Guilt is particularly low vibrational and it can be easy to ruminate on our actions and stay in this space. The aim is to break the spiral by listening to our conflicting parts. For this I found the book on Internal Family Systems "Self-Therapy" by Jay Early and "Healing The Shame That Binds You" by John Bradshaw both informative ad practical.

Running and meditation for example are coping mechanisms. We need to express for the body to recognize that we have heard the boundary. We don't need to be aggressive, just kind and firm.

Whilst I was in Egypt I went on a balloon trip over the Valley of the Kings. It was breathtaking as the sunrise was making it's way gently across the hazy hillsides with the Nile's reflection in the background. Just another morning of quiet beauty and simplicity without nature needing any notion of ostentatiousness to impart her majesty.

As we were about to touch down, I observed a particularly interesting demonstration of leadership. There were a small group of Chinese tourists in our group who clearly didn't speak English very well at all. Before we had entered the balloon, the captain had detailed the safety instructions about how we'd land. In their excitement, this group had given him the impression that they had understood but now that we were landing it was quite clear that it wasn't the case and they weren't moving into landing position. The captain raised his voice as he gave the instructions a second and a third time, clearly becoming very annoyed. I could feel both the worry for their safety and the indignation in his voice at his authority being ignored. He very quickly indicated to another person to show them non-verbally, re-focused himself on the landing, and moments later we were touching down safely. Moments later as we were secure he couldn't help but repeat his dismay, firmly and clearly explaining what they should have done. Then he smiled really broadly and offered them a high-five which spoke so loudly of "*no hard feelings*", a peace offering which was accepted, asking them subsequently if they had enjoyed the ride in a really authentic way. A nice example of heart-centred leadership I thought "*I need to say this because you overstepped my boundary but I know we can get past it*". Beautiful.

There is a lot of latent anger within companies and indeed society as a whole. It comes from years of suppressing those unmet needs and lack of verbalisation of frustrations. Of allowing ourselves to be victims of both systems and other's projections, but also from us trying to control events when they don't match our idea of how they should be. This needs to be externalized in order to heal and so we can collectively make the choice to build better, more cohesive systems that respond to our individual need for self-realization and also collective unity. Essentially anger is a very powerful source of creativity when we have the courage to recognize what is not working for us and initiate change. The first step is to go through it in order to get to a place of forgiveness. We have all used fear and control mechanisms of some kind in the past so it is vital not to stay in a posture of duality and righteousness blaming others or the organizations themselves. Don't stay with it because indeed the resentment will impact you personally, simply respect yourself by moving away from anything which doesn't match with your values or is detrimental to your well-being. It is part of a system that we all maintained and can now choose to redefine. Let's stop pretending it doesn't exist and instead use our vital energy positively to co-construct systems and organizations which raise rather than reduce humanity.

Courage and Compassion

Heart-centred leadership is most certainly not for the faint of heart but it is available to all of us if we wish to take even a first step in that direction. Courage and compassion both come from that same place, our hearts. They propel us into action where we would otherwise absolve our desires or responsibilities to others.

I believe we should always look at the meaning of words that we use. They are so powerful in their resonance, so I found myself pondering over compassion, which I broke into com and passion. Passion is what you share with the world, what stirs your soul, the real you. We talk a lot about the importance of being. Passion is what comes of the actions you take when you are truly enjoying and being in alignment with your joys and gifts. It is our being "experienced". What is interesting is that the prefix 'com' represents "together", "with", "in association" and with "intense force" i.e. "completely". So it can ultimately be seen as a word that expresses our need to join together to experience collectively who we are, with the whole of our beings.

The dictionary definition of compassion rather suggests a place of pity which is a shame. When we show compassion, the connection from our heart centres causes us to wish to support, talk, and share with others, the focus of our compassion. Yes we can make choices to do these things but some of the most communicative and humane aspects of our being are also our smiles, our light and our humour, our songs, our touch, and many of the other 'small' things that we can forget are absolutely crucial for us to function in an empathic, communal way. These communicate our passion much better!

Compassion is a function of our ability to guide our actions towards the greater good. A willingness to discover ourselves through and with others. To know that their wellbeing is also linked to ours.

That we can be whatever we want and it detracts from no-one else when we make choices from the heart. There is room for win-win when we connect with others. We can alternatively be in a place of hate, fear, or negativity. It is a choice which will reflect in your state of mind and wellbeing, which also drives us to create from a much higher place.

Compassion moves us to connect, to share, to be with, to accept others. It is a pathway to a place of a higher level of love that we can attain. We have a choice of who to be in any moment with respect to an event. So next time you find yourself in the face of sadness or chaos, remember the different contributions you can make by adding your lightness. Empathize, don't sympathize. Don't get in the hole with the person, it doesn't help to lift them. They need your compassion in the positive sense, your strength, your example of hope not pity in order to see the possibility of shifting out of their current difficulty.

Courage in the face of risk and adversity for a heart-centred leader invites us to be that sparkling big hearted person that embraces life and all of its possibility. It will inspire others into action, in togetherness. Fundamentally, share your passion and ultimately your compassion for life with others in the strongest way your gifts allow.

What if life was just a practice run, wouldn't you take more risks to follow your heart and create in order to discover the most magnificent version of yourself? Imagine the power and alignment of a team or community all working in this way?

When we move through the feelings of fear and pride we arrive at another heart-centred quality, courage. It's important to keep this fact in mind as we work with developing creativity and trying new behaviours. It takes a little exploration and practice to reawaken our passions.

> *"Remain true to yourself, but move ever upward toward greater consciousness and greater love! At the summit you will find yourselves united with all those who, from every direction, have made the same ascent. For everything that rises must converge."* Pierre Teilhard de Chardin

All human beings are creative, although we express our creativity in different ways, whether its finding a new solution to a problem, an idea, a way of doing or expressing something, or more traditionally through art and design. To come full circle, when we truly discover our sovereignty, this immediately encourages us to question our choices and the reality that we are creating. Are we making choices which are in line with our highest good? Are we collectively making the best choices that we can? How might we use our courage to co-create more effectively?

Rather than being in a state of negativity and blame, we can look at our part in the systems around us and ask ourselves whether we are reinforcing something which is positive for well-being or upholding a status quo which does not serve us any longer?

Just because we made a choice in the past it does not mean to say that we have to remain with it. What was good yesterday, may not be today. We can stand back to be the observer of the current situation without being pulled into the drama. Indeed, as we learn to surrender to life's flow we see that our strength lies in our ability to see what is and make more loving choices as a consequence. This includes loving ourselves and therefore not accepting situations which are not in alignment with our true self, our values, our well-being. This is standing in your truth and letting yourself into your life! When we remove what is not in line with our true self, we often encounter many synchronicities which help to support us in experiencing our real truth. Thank the contrast of the old system or environment which helped us to recognize what we are not, what we do not want and therefore empowers us to share who we wish to be. Let these systems be reference points without attaching to them. This is why it is so important not to be caught up in fear or anger because we then get caught up in the story rather than using our energy and choices more wisely for ourselves in the direction of truth and positivity.

The practice of Appreciative Inquiry is based around the principles of identifying and valuing the past and present strengths that we have in order to co-create through discovery, dream and design. It links the identification of peak experiences, with positive beliefs, to channel the energy of these positives into designing and taking steps towards a future containing more positive potential. In doing so, it strives to find the best in people, our organizations and the environment around us. We can start by giving this gift to ourselves.

As we inquire around what we wish to create together, the question of transparency is paramount. If everyone is to be involved then everyone can engage and participate in creating the framework or environment within which the new will emerge. The rules should be understandable and visible to all. When we are sovereign we choose to engage, we choose to give our energy to projects that are important to us. In doing so we flourish but we cannot do so if there is no transparency in the way we operate together, our creative energy is diverted.

In the same way, I find that as we progress on the spiritual path, we also try to integrate more simplicity into our lives. This is not a question of shying away from complexity, on the contrary. We can see its reality today but it no longer feels like a necessity. We can take the complex and remove the superfluous from it. When we have found a sense of lightness in ourselves, the last thing we want to do is to weigh that down again and over-burden ourselves with distorted, convoluted solutions. Going directly to the essence or essential in what we do just seems the most logical and obvious course of action for a resilient, maintainable solution, especially between many co-creators. We over-complicate so many parts of our lives, which sometimes seems to provide either distraction or a way of proving our credibility. We don't need either. As we strip away that which is not essential we find clarity and peace of mind. There is less likelihood of mis-communication and drama, leaving more time for connecting and indeed progressing together in a positive space of joy.

CONCLUSION

I believe in personal responsibility, for our emotions, our behaviour and the reality we co-create. I am the whole range of emotions and my body feels the whole range. What I choose to do with that, using it for destruction or for learning and a higher purpose is my question. It is the only question I need to ask myself. Am I choosing from a place of love or a place of fear and therefore who am I being in respect to my current context?

We are never separate from others, we never were, but now our increased consciousness is making us blatantly aware of the impact of what we put back into the collective conscious. If we are saying and doing from a place of alignment then it is always the right thing. Our true self doesn't want to hurt others so honor your sovereignty from the highest place by making choices with love and integrity. Find your story through your contrast, then by following your truth through the courage of your heart you will be propelled forward to rediscover your greatness. This is all we were ever intended to do. How can there be wrong in that? It is all perfect. As we lift our being, we catalyse others to do the same.

We have all the hard skills we need, they are still useful but they are not the way to evolve. In a complex environment we cannot function by continuing to accumulate in our minds. We are simply overloaded. There is so much information and so many options that we become paralysed and the transformation of our organizations with them. Connecting with our true selves means unlearning, putting down our mental maps and being open to the fact that it is ok for our minds not to know. Our true self does know what is right for us. To get to this place, much of the work that we need to do is preventative, ensuring we have the right thoughts and behaviours in place so that we can take optimal actions as events arise. This takes a huge change in mindset. To make space for feeling and creating using all of our being, our wholeness. To want to meet others in the middle in authenticity, leaving space for their wholeness to also express.

The heart-centred leader says *"what got me here is perfect, this is my current reality. I see and accept it with clarity. I take responsibility for it. What do I want to do with it now? What feels like the right action for me and the collective? How can I best use my gifts? What is your reality and what do you feel is the way forward? What are your gifts? How can we use this to emerge something which is bigger than each of us individually? That lifts rather than lowers us and the collective? Then let's vision together. How can we take the first step? Are we willing to make this work? Then we can trust that we will find a way together through dialogue and co-operative action"*.

With higher consciousness we will eventually arrive at the stage where teams function with enough trust and intuition that they *know* that the right thing will emerge from their collective actions. Their progress will not be frozen by fear and the light frameworks in place will offer them the opportunity to co-create without judgement of 'mistakes'. This a time of reality, community and for each and every one of us to lead from the heart in order to rediscover our true selves and in doing so offer those leadership skills to living a vibrant life in communion with others and for the betterment of all.

AFTERWORD

I believe very strongly in the idea that through self-leadership practices, everyone can find and share their own truth whilst also respecting and interacting with others. In researching these different practices, I came to the conclusion that this is essentially finding God within oneself and also seeing it in others. Given my belief in free will, I chose not to mix any discussion about God within the text to allow you to decide for yourself. My authenticity compels me to share this journey with you. The practice of reconnecting to one's truth quite naturally encourages us to question what our soul is and how our purpose relates to others. This is my story :

I was lucky to have parents who gave me the freedom to explore my gifts and values. As a teen some of my family were practicing Church of England and others not at all. As a somewhat rebellious teen and young adult, in the sense of '*I'll make my own mind up*', I went out into the world discovering one face of God after another. My social environment was ethnically diverse and my father made a principle of building bridges to different cultures. Why would one vision of God be right and not another? I had a sense that God existed out there but more as an external entity whose form was of little importance to me.

I set out on my path to discover the meaning of self-leadership through both my professional activities as a head of a learning practice for an international organization, and also for personal reasons following a difficult period in my life. My encounters and experiences unfolded into what I saw in hindsight as leading me back to the knowing of God's existence. In searching for examples of community, in understanding how we can take responsibility for our health, our beliefs, our relationships, I was led to a moment where I found myself laughing with joy. I had come to my realisation of the existence of a God who is pure love, who does not judge and gives us the freedom to create whatever we desire. The irony was that if you had told me to believe that, I wouldn't have been convinced. In allowing my story to unfold and searching with an open mind, my free will had been respected. There is no need to impose a truth, it just is. *"How deliciously intelligent this all is!"* I concluded. This is mine. I respect yours.

I understand, having been through the process, how important integrity is in allowing each and every person to decide. I abhor having anything forced upon me so I will always keep the approaches that I talk about separate, even if this can at times be hard. I do believe that there is a deeper dimension to them, especially when we look at the perfection of contrast. The more I look inwards and in writing this book, I am sharing my belief, not that there is a right or wrong way to be, but from a place of deep trust that when we connect to our truths we simply make more humane choices both individually and therefore collectively. I guess God just wishes, like any loving parent, that we would make better choices for our well-being! It is all about being awake to and respecting the interdependency of choice that comes with unity consciousness.

> *"Someday, after mastering the winds, the waves, the tides and gravity, we shall harness for God the energies of love, and then, for a second time in the history of the world, man will have discovered fire."* Pierre Teilhard de Chardin

BIBLIOGRAPHY

Benner, Joseph. "The Impersonal Life", Timeless Wisdom Collection, 2016

Born, Paul. "Deepening Community: Finding Joy in Chaotic Times", Berrett Koehler, 2014

Bradshaw, John."Healing The Shame That Binds You", Health Communications Inc., 2005

Cameron, Julia "The artist's Way", Penguin Putnam Inc., 2002

Demartini, John F. "The Values Factor", Berkley, 2013

Early, Jay. "Self-Therapy", Pattern System Books, 2009

Hawkins, David R. "Letting Go: The Pathway To Surrender", Hay House Inc, 2012

Haas, Simon. "The Book of Dharma: Making Enlightened Choices", Veda Wisdom Books, 2013

Laloux, Frédéric. "Reinventing Organizations", Nelson Parker, 2014

Lipmanowicz, Henri & McCandless, Keith. "The Surprising Power of Liberating Structures"

Monbourquette, Jean. "Apprivoiser Son Ombre : Le Côté Mal Aimé de Soi", Points Vivre, Editions Bayard 2011, Editions Novalis inc., 2010

Senge, Peter M., Scharmer, Otto C., Jaworski, Joseph, Flowers, Betty Sue. "Presence: Exploring Profound Change in People, Organizations, and Society", Doubleday, 2004

Truman, Karol K. "Feelings Buried Alive Never Die"

Walsch, Neale Donald. "Conversations With God", Hodder & Stoughton, 1999

ABOUT THE AUTHOR

Nadia is passionate about people, their stories, the strength to be gained from their diversity and their capacity to evolve. As such, she has come to specialize in the fields of culture, personal development, self-direction and co-creation. As a pragmatist she strives to achieve self-help and sustainable solutions. Ones that connect head and heart!

She has travelled extensively, and worked in a variety of business contexts during her career, from creative, to highly analytical, to people-focused, in both public and private sectors. Consequently, she has developed a talent for finding synergies across disciplines in order to emerge new possibilities, so she invariably finds herself serving as a catalyst for change. The main? strength of her experience, however, lies in the teams with whom she's had the enormous pleasure to work with and lead, and her network of fabulous people from all walks of life that she continuously enjoys growing with!

When she's not travelling, she lives in Paris with her two children.